The Language of TESOL and Bilingual Education

The Language of Education

KEY TERMS AND CONCEPTS IN TEACHING AND LEARNING

Series Editor

William F. McComas (*Parks Family Distinguished Professor of Science Education, University of Arkansas, Fayetteville, AR, USA*)

VOLUME 4

The titles published in this series are listed at *brill.com/tloe*

The Language of TESOL and Bilingual Education

An Expanded Glossary of Key Terms and Concepts

By

Alissa Blair, Anneliese Cannon, Janet Penner-Williams and
Roseli M. Matos Franco

BRILL

LEIDEN | BOSTON

Cover illustration: iStock.com/wildpixel

All chapters in this book have undergone peer review.

The Library of Congress Cataloging-in-Publication Data is available online at https://catalog.loc.gov

Typeface for the Latin, Greek, and Cyrillic scripts: "Brill". See and download: brill.com/brill-typeface.

ISSN 2666-0121
ISBN 978-90-04-69206-0 (paperback)
ISBN 978-90-04-69207-7 (hardback)
ISBN 978-90-04-69208-4 (e-book)
DOI 10.1163/9789004692084

Copyright 2024 by Alissa Blair, Anneliese Cannon, Janet Penner-Williams and Roseli M. Matos Franco
Published by Koninklijke Brill NV, Leiden, The Netherlands.
Koninklijke Brill NV incorporates the imprints Brill, Brill Nijhoff, Brill Schöningh, Brill Fink, Brill mentis, Brill Wageningen Academic, Vandenhoeck & Ruprecht, Böhlau and V&R unipress.
Koninklijke Brill NV reserves the right to protect this publication against unauthorized use. Requests for re-use and/or translations must be addressed to Koninklijke Brill NV via brill.com or copyright.com.

This book is printed on acid-free paper and produced in a sustainable manner.

Contents

Foreword   IX
    Socorro G. Herrera
Preface   XI

Academic Language   1
Affective Filter Hypothesis   3
Allophones   4
Assets-Based Pedagogies   5
Assimilation and Acculturation   7
Audio-Lingual Method (ALM)   8
Bilingual Education Act   9
Bilingualism (models of)   10
Bilinguals (types of)   11
Castañeda v. Pickard (1981)   12
Code Switching   13
Cognates   14
Common European Framework of Reference (CEFR) for Language   15
Common Underlying Proficiency (CPU)   16
Communicative Competence   17
Communicative Language Teaching (CLT)   18
Community Language Learning (CLL)   19
Content and Language Integrated Learning (CLIL)   20
Critical Period Hypothesis (CPH)   21
Critical Perspectives and Pedagogies   22
Discourse   25
Disproportionality   26
English as a Second Language (ESL)   28
English as Lingua Franca (ELF)   29
English for Specific Purposes (ESP)   30
English Language Proficiency (ELP)   31
English Language Proficiency Standards   33
English Learner (ELS)   34
Error Correction   35
Figurative Language   37
Fossilization   38
Genre   39
Grammar Translation Method (GTM)   40
Heritage Language Learners   41

Homonyms   42
Individual Learner Differences   43
Input Hypothesis   45
Intensive English Programs (IEPs)   46
Interlanguage   47
L1   48
Language Domains   49
Language Functions   51
Language Loss   52
Language Planning   53
Language Policy   54
Language Revitalization   55
Language Transfer   56
Lau v. Nichols (1974)   57
Linguistics   58
Long-Term English Learner (L-TEL)   59
Metalinguistic Awareness   60
Migrant Education   61
Monitor Hypothesis   63
Morphology   64
Native American Languages Act   65
Native Speaker (NS) and Nonnative Speaker (NNS)   66
Natural Approach (NA)   67
Natural Order Hypothesis   68
Newcomer Program   69
Noticing Hypothesis   70
Notional Functional Method   71
Orthography   72
Phonological Awareness and Phonemic Awareness   73
Phonology   74
Plyler v. Doe (1982)   75
Pragmatics   76
Program Models   77
Scaffolding   80
Seal of Biliteracy   81
Second Language Acquisition Hypothesis   82
Semantics   83
Sheltered Instruction   84
Silent Period   85
Silent Way   86
Sociocultural Theory   87

Stages of Second Language Acquisition   88
Students with Limited or Interrupted Formal Education (SLIFE)   89
Suggestopedia   90
Syntax   91
Systemic Functional Linguistics (SFL)   92
Task-Based Language Teaching   93
Total Physical Response (TPR)   94
Translanguaging   95
Universal Grammar (UG)   96
U.S. School Procedures for Identification and Services for English Learners   97
Vocabulary Teaching and Learning   98
World Englishes   99

Appendix A: TESOL and Bilingual Education Organizations   101

Foreword

As a teacher *educator* at a research university, I have for many years collaborated with the authors of this text. These collaborations have spanned a range of endeavors, including: (a) the development and delivery of U.S. Department of Education Title II and VII National Professional Development Projects; (b) the creation of differentiated and nuanced curricula for educators of multilingual learners (MLs); and (c) the pursuit of research and publications addressing critical issues in TESOL and teacher education within increasingly diverse and complex learning environments. Each of these authors is a scholar, bringing a wealth of knowledge and expertise to bear on asset-based teaching and learning, bilingual and dual language education, and TESOL-related research in the United States (U.S.) and internationally. Their commitment extends to advocating for innovative practices that benefit multilingual children and adults. Over the course of their careers, they have amassed extensive experience in researching and collaborating with educators across a variety of settings.

Despite the strides made in providing educators with targeted professional learning focused on asset-based instruction for multilingual learners over the past decade, research indicates that many educators still seek further professional learning opportunities. These opportunities are needed to effectively address the complexities of classrooms characterized by diverse races and ethnicities, cultures, and home languages. In particular, a limited number of educators feel confident using methods or pivotal strategies for asset-based instruction and literacy development. Not surprisingly then, few of these educators regularly engage with language that brings defensibility to their practice and language that will support them in interacting with MLs and other stakeholders. As a result, they may possess limited awareness of the funds of knowledge they might leverage in accelerating student engagement, progress, and persistence.

In this volume, the authors delve into the foundational principles and contemporary terminology underpinning their field. They examine concepts related to culture, community, funds of knowledge, literacy development, assets-based praxis, nuanced perspectives on language ownership, and the critical distinction between equity and equality in language teaching. Further, the authors tackle emergent concepts like translanguaging, in ways that are comprehensible yet elucidating, informative and at the same time historically contextualized.

I champion the value of this much needed and clarifying text, which elucidates the nomenclature and terminology relevant to TESOL and bilingual education. This "lingua franca" of the profession remains too often unfamiliar to many educators or incompletely understood in instructional contexts where the assets of differential acculturation and bilingualism are not maximized as matters of best practice, grounded in the findings of meaningful research.

Readers of this book will discover the range of research and resources for understanding more about both the fundamentals and the horizons of TESOL and bilingual education as well as informed recommendations for promising practices with MLs. I hope that this book will become a primer for practitioners, teacher educators, and professional developers, helping professionals across a variety of instructional contexts to learn, teach, and practice racially, culturally, and linguistically responsive education.

Socorro G. Herrera

Preface

The fields of TESOL (Teaching English to Speakers of Other Languages) and bilingual education are fundamentally concerned with language teaching and learning. How fitting, then, to apply a language lens to these fields and make the most common terms transparent and palpable to an educator audience. As the renowned literary critic Mikhail Bakhtin (1981) notes, "all words have the taste of a profession, a genre, a tendency, a party, a particular work, a particular person, a generation, an age group, the day and hour" (p. 293). Indeed, the terminology related to TESOL and bilingual education, as with so many disciplines and topic areas, is dynamic, nuanced, and ever evolving. This is particularly the case as teaching and research in relation to multilingual learners continue to expand. As a result, consensus on fundamental terms is often elusive. For example, how we refer to learners of a language or how languages are even referred to, reflect a certain learning context as well underlying assumptions about language development. In this volume, the authors have not attempted to take on these issues, but rather, to help equip educators and education students with key terminology so that they navigate the field, particularly as instructional contexts become more linguistically and culturally diverse in the U.S. and globally.

This encyclopedic reference, *The Language of TESOL and Bilingual Education: An Expanded Glossary of Key Terms and Concepts* is an attempt to provide clarity and context for readers to feel more comfortable acquiring words with "the taste of the profession." This volume is not meant to be exhaustive but rather a starting point to develop a better understanding of big ideas that often circulate in everyday teacher talk, education policy, and academic articles. Unlike traditional dictionaries or encyclopedias, this volume offers both succinct definitions on the first line of each entry to serve as a quick reference, as well as extended definitions to develop a more comprehensive understanding of each term. In most entries, the term's origin is mentioned as well as current usage and even how the term might be contested. Most importantly, each entry includes connections to practice. These connections aid in the shift from being able to simply recognize a term, to applying it in everyday circumstances. Finally, many entries make mention of other terms in the volume to encourage further reading and to recognize connections between concepts.

The intended audience of this volume is any practitioner, student, or scholar hoping to deepen their familiarity with TESOL and bilingual education. With this resource, current TESOL or bilingual education practitioners or administrators might benefit from fine-tuning their understanding and use of terms and related considerations for practice. Undergraduate students or graduate students studying TESOL and bilingual education will benefit from a resource to complement scholarly reading that assumes familiarity with common terms and concepts. While many of the terms and definitions are specific to a U.S. education context, international students, or educators, especially those new to publishing, studying, or working in the United States or similar context, would benefit from the nuance provided in this rendering of common terms. Finally, teacher educators in TESOL and bilingual education might suggest or draw from this volume to support student learning, and collaborators of TESOL and bilingual education scholars might wish to confer with this resource to complement certain related or different term usage in their respective fields.

Careful consideration and consensus were given to the selection of terms and concepts. Initial terms were generated through brainstorming, followed by a rigorous feedback process involving scholars and practitioners within and outside the United States. The co-authors, who have extensive experience teaching English and other languages in different regions such as the Americas, Europe, and East Asia, utilized their knowledge to create clear, practical, and substantial definitions by drawing on their insights into common pedagogical challenges and misconceptions in TESOL and bilingual education theory and practice. For the sake of readability, several terms are used interchangeably within and across entries (e.g., student learning English as an additional language/English learner; additional language/L2, etc.).

In conclusion, with a sense of humility and an appreciation for the intricacies of language acquisition and usage, this volume is presented to readers with the aim of achieving clarity while also fostering a continual quest for greater clarity. The best use of a resource such as this is having conversations with others and adding to its pages one's own entries and nuance to terms. To return to the words of Bakhtin (1981), "the word in language is half someone else's." Said differently, we must hear a word, use it, understand what experiences necessitate it, and from there, "one must take the word, and make it one's own" (p. 206).

Bakhtin, M. M. (1981). The dialogic imagination: Four essays by M. M. Bakhtin. In M. Holquist (Ed.), *Four essays by M. M. Bakhtin* (C. Emerson & M. Holquist, Trans.). University of Texas.

Academic language encompasses the often discipline-specific ways language is used in speaking, listening, reading, writing, viewing, and interacting while learning in classroom-based settings and beyond.

Academic language spans multiple dimensions, or levels of language use (Bailey, 2007; Gottlieb & Ernst-Slavit, 2014), including the word/phrase dimension (pertaining to general, specialized, and technical words and expressions, multiple meanings of words, nominalizations and idiomatic expressions), the sentence dimension (which pertains to syntax, sentence and clause type, and prepositional phrases), and the discourse dimension (having to do with text type, genre expectations, organization of text or speech, cohesion, coherence, and voice) (Gibbons, 2002). These dimensions are important for educators to develop a robust understanding of academic language rather than narrowly associate academic language with the teaching of vocabulary alone.

In part, the term academic language has its origins in the distinction made by Jim Cummins (2008) between Basic Interpersonal Communication Skills (BICS) and Cognitive Academic Language Proficiency (CALP). It is important for educators to understand that the distinction is not a basis for treating academic language as more "cognitively demanding" or other registers of language use as more "basic." Rather, the distinction can help educators understand the time it takes to develop academic language proficiency and the need for academic language to be explicitly taught. Research estimates that in school settings it can take children 4–7 years become proficient in academic language compared with the estimated 3–5 years necessary to develop oral language skills (Hakuta et al., 2000; Thomas & Collier, 1997).

In the U.S., the College and Career Readiness Standards prioritize teaching academic language explicitly by emphasizing such skills as analysis, making claims, providing evidence, and reading complex, non-fiction texts (Common Core Standards Initiative, 2021). Strategies that support academic language learning are those that embed academic language teaching into content, explicitly teach vocabulary, and focus on sentence structures and genre expectations commonly used in written and spoken academic language.

At the post-secondary level, academic language still plays a prominent role. Coxhead (Coxhead, 2022; School of Linguistics and Applied Language Studies, n.d.) developed the Academic Word List (AWL), previously known as University Word List that consists of approximately 570-word families and 3000 words total, including derivations like affixes and suffixes. Developers and users of this list recommend explicit instruction in academic vocabulary that derives mostly from Greek and Latin even at the collegiate level.

In sum, very few scholars or practitioners would dispute that there are unique academic language and literacy demands associated with school-based learning. However, scholars have offered various critiques of the notion of academic language. One critique is that academic language reinforces a dichotomy between school-based and non-school-based language, which is a misrepresentation of the complexities of the varied social registers of language that students come to school with (Haneda, 2014). Others argue that academic language perpetuates an unequal dichotomy between language that is often used in white, monolingual cultures and other, equally valid forms of language (Flores & Rosa, 2015) and that, in turn, gives advantage and privilege to middle- and upper-class students who are more likely to be given opportunities to practice and excel at these styles of language.

See also: Language Domains, Systemic Functional Linguistics (SFL), Vocabulary Teaching and Learning.

Bailey, A. L. (Ed.). (2007). *The language demands of school: Putting academic English to the test*. Yale University Press.
Common Core State Standards Initiative. (2020). *Key shifts in English language arts*. https://www.thecorestandards.org/other-resources/key-shifts-in-english-language-arts/
Coxhead, A. (2000). A new academic word list. *TESOL Quarterly, 34*(2), 213–238.
Cummins, J. (2008). BICS and CALP: Empirical and theoretical status of the distinction. In B. Street & N. H. Hornberger (Eds.), *Encyclopedia of language and education* (2nd ed., pp. 71–83). Springer.
Flores, N., & Rosa, J. (2015). Undoing appropriateness: Raciolinguistic ideologies and language diversity in education. *Harvard Educational Review, 85*(2), 149–171.
Gibbons, P. (2002). *Scaffolding language, scaffolding learning*. Heinemann.
Gottlieb, M., & Ernst-Slavit, G. (2014). *Academic language in diverse classrooms: Definitions and contexts*. Corwin Press.
Hakuta, K., Butler, Y. G., & Witt, D. (2000). *How long does it take for English learners to attain proficiency?* Linguistic Minority Research Institute. https://files.eric.ed.gov/fulltext/ED443275.pdf
Haneda, M. (2014). From academic language to academic communication: Building on English learners' resources. *Linguistics and Education, 26*, 126–135.
School of Linguistics and Applied Language Studies. (n.d.). *The academic word list*. https://www.wgtn.ac.nz/lals/resources/academicwordlist
Thomas, W. P., & Collier, V. (1997). *School effectiveness for language minority students: NCBE Resource Collection Series, No. 9*. National Clearinghouse for Bilingual Education. https://files.eric.ed.gov/fulltext/ED436087.pdf

Affective Filter Hypothesis refers to the influence of the learner's state of mind in acquiring language, including emotions such as motivation, self-confidence, and anxiety.

The Affective Filter Hypothesis by Krashen (1982) acknowledges the role of affect and emotion and specifically how it can impede the process of acquiring an additional language. Further, less constructive emotions, such as fear or embarrassment, can form a barrier or "filter" to effective language learning. Krashen stressed that teachers play an important role in setting up a low-stress and motivational environment for language learners. Because the affective filter is related to his other ideas that languages are acquired (an unconscious process), learning environments should be "just right" with the amount of comprehensible input and keep the active filter low.

While other researchers have also examined the role that affective variables like motivation play in language learning (Dörnyei & Schmidt, 2001), there are critiques of concepts like motivation or the affective filter. For example, Norton-Pierce (1995) argues that we cannot isolate an affective filter or factors like motivation from the larger social context. Instead, according to Norton Pierce, a learner's sense of identity and investment are shaped by the environment, as well as the people and power relations at play in any given setting (workplace, classroom, etc.). She advocates for teachers giving learners opportunities to reflect on when and where they feel comfort or, conversely, inhibition speaking the target language and to reflect on how identity and power factor into their feelings and sense of agency in expressing themselves.

Teachers can consider students' mental state by striving to create learning environments that are low-stress, welcoming, and tactful in error-correction. Teachers can also refrain from overemphasizing motivation solely as an attribute of the learner, and explore with students which situations increase their investment and positive sense of self as a language learner.

See also: Comprehensible Input Hypothesis, Error Correction, Fossilization, Second Language Acquisition Hypothesis

Dörnyei, Z., & Schmidt, R. (Eds.). (2001). *Motivation and second language acquisition* (Vol. 23). National Foreign Language Resource Center.
Krashen, S. (1982). *Principles and practice in second language acquisition*. Oxford University Press.
Peirce, B. N. (1995). Social identity, investment, and language learning. *TESOL Quarterly*, 29(1), 9–31.

Allophones are different pronunciations of the same phoneme, which make a difference in how a word is pronounced.

Pronunciation of a phoneme depends on its position in the word—whether it is a beginning or ending sound and what sound precedes or follows it. Despite the slight difference in pronunciation, the meaning of the phoneme is the same. Allophones came about through phonemes assimilating to nearby sounds. When English speakers say, "Keys cost" The /k/ sound in *keys* has the tongue farther forward due to assimilation to the position of the tongue for /i/. The /k/ sound in *cost* has the tongue further back in the mouth assimilating to the position for the following sound of /u/. Individuals listening to a language they know well will ignore allophonic variations.

Some phonemes such as /t/ are more complex than /k/. The phoneme /t/ has six variations involving physical differences. The affricative /t/ sound is produced in a similar manner to the voiceless alveopalatal affricative /t/. Young children noticing this similarity may therefore spell *train* as *chain*.

Allophones are of special interest to learners and teachers of English since often when learning a language, students hear the allophone variation and do not immediately classify it as belonging to the same phoneme. The cognitive load of paying attention to each allophone is similar to the cognitive load of processing rapid speech. Consequently, English learners may perceive fluent or "native" speakers as speaking at a rapid pace (Freeman & Freeman, 2014).

For a more in-depth examination of allophonic contrasts at different ages for second language learners see Shea (2014).

See also: Phonological Awareness and Phonemic Awareness, Phonology.

Freeman, D. E., & Freeman, Y. S. (2014). *Essential linguistics: What teachers need to know to teach ESL, reading, spelling, grammar* (2nd ed.). Heinemann.

Shea, C. E. (2014). Second language learners and the variable speech signal. *Frontiers in Psychology, 5,* 1–3.

Assets-Based Pedagogies refer to approaches that treat students' linguistic and cultural heritage as valuable resources for learning.

Assets-based approaches vary from deficit or difference-based approaches that position students' backgrounds as limitations or barriers to assimilating into the school community or society at large. Assets-based pedagogies are not specific to the fields of TESOL or bilingual education alone, but rather, have been applied to the education of linguistically and culturally diverse students more broadly. Nonetheless, assets-based pedagogies are especially relevant for teaching multilingual learners because of the rich linguistic and cultural resources they bring to learning.

Funds of knowledge form the basis of assets-based pedagogies. Funds of knowledge refer to the skills, experiences, jobs, social networks, and histories among families and communities that provide students with social, cultural, and cognitive resources that teachers can leverage to enrich school-based learning (Moll et al., 1992). Teachers can learn about families' funds of knowledge through home visits and other conversations that situate the teacher as a learner. Learning about families' funds of knowledge is important because it can help disrupt deficit views of linguistically and culturally diverse families and embrace students' varying linguistic and cultural practices from an assets-based perspective.

Culturally relevant pedagogy is based on recognizing students' linguistic and cultural practices as assets and as the starting point for pursuing academic excellence and developing critical consciousness. This pedagogy is *relevant* in the sense that it "empowers students intellectually, socially, emotionally, and politically by using cultural referents to impart knowledge, skills, and attitudes" (Ladson-Billings, 1994, p. 18). Rather than turning an eye to students' racial, ethnic, and linguistic identities, a culturally relevant teacher helps students construct knowledge and see themselves as capable contributors to their communities and beyond (Ladson-Billings, 1994).

Culturally responsive pedagogy is similar to culturally relevant pedagogy in affirming linguistic and cultural diversity and emphasizes *responding* to students' unique cultures and strengths in order to effectively teach them. A teacher with culturally responsive practices relies on "the cultural knowledge, prior experiences, frames of reference, and performance styles of ethnically diverse students to make learning encounters more relevant and effective for them" (Gay, 2000, p. 29). In this sense, a culturally relevant teacher might organize instruction so students see themselves reflected in the curriculum, situate the exploration of school-based topics in familiar experiences and cultural references, and make space for students to examine issues through their own and other viewpoints.

Culturally sustaining pedagogy, like culturally relevant pedagogy and culturally responsive pedagogy, supports using students' diverse backgrounds as assets for classroom learning. However, culturally sustaining pedagogy furthers this idea by placing importance on *sustaining*, that is, "perpetuating and fostering linguistic, literate, and cultural pluralism as part of the democratic project of schooling" (Paris, 2012, p. 95). In this approach, students' and communities' funds of knowledge are not valued solely to facilitate school-based learning, but worthy of sustaining for their own selves and a multicultural society. Culturally sustaining practices include teaching students about a variety of linguistic styles and modes of expression, making connections to literature, current events, and issues of importance, developing tools of critique to address social injustices, and partnering with families to help sustain home language practices and cultural traditions (Paris & Alim, 2017).

It is important to note that assets-based approaches cannot be reduced to a uniform set of teaching practices. Assets-based practices entails a mindset, that is, a view of teaching and learning that considers the "social, emotional, cognitive, political, and cultural dimensions of every student" and the development of critical consciousness so students take active and productive roles in both classroom learning and the pursuit of their educational goals more broadly (Powell et al., 2016, p. 6).

See also: Critical Perspectives and Pedagogies

Gay, G. (2000). *Culturally responsive teaching: Theory, research, and practice.* Teachers College Press.
Ladson-Billings, G. (1994). *The dreamkeepers: Successful teachers of African American children.* Jossey-Bass.
Moll, L. C., Amanti, C., Neff, D., & Gonzalez, N. (1992). Funds of knowledge for teaching: Using a qualitative approach to connect homes and classrooms. *Theory Into Practice, 31*(2), 132–141.
Paris, D. (2012). Culturally sustaining pedagogy: A needed change in stance, terminology, and practice. *Educational Researcher, 41*(3), 93–97.
Paris, D., & Alim, H. S. (Eds.). (2017). *Culturally sustaining pedagogies: Teaching and learning for justice in a changing world.* Teachers College Press.
Powell, R., Cantrell, S. C., Malo-Juvera, V., & Correll, P. (2016). Operationalizing culturally responsive instruction: Preliminary findings of CRIOP research. *Teachers College Record, 118*(1), 1–46.

Assimilation and acculturation are terms often used in education and other fields to represent how immigrants adapt to new surroundings and how aspects of the surrounding culture may also undergo changes in response.

Assimilation has been expected of immigrants to the U.S. throughout the history of U.S. immigration. Immigrants have been expected to assimilate to the dominant U.S. culture including abandoning their native tongue and becoming proficient in English. The goal of assimilation was to have immigrants fully adopt cultural norms, customs and language to the country they immigrated to. This concept was often referred to as the "melting pot" paradigm and played a prominent role in the primary and secondary education systems throughout various waves of immigration. During the process of assimilation, the target language group typically occupies a higher social status compared with the second language learning group. Assimilation, however, is only one of the integration strategies that impacts second language learning (Shumann, 1986).

Acculturation, in contrast, as an integration strategy, places emphasis on maintaining one's norms, customs and home language while also embracing the cultural norms, customs and the language of the host country. The culture immigrants brought to the country is valued and maintained while new norms, customs, and the national language are learned. This process contributes to individuals who are bilingual and bicultural. The metaphor for acculturation is the "salad bowl" image where the two cultures and linguistic expertise coexist and are viewed as assets (Gollnick & Chin, 2013). The student does not lose their native language and customs but instead gains a new repertoire derived from the country they have adopted.

See also: Language Loss, Language Revitalization.

Gollnick, D. M., & Chin, P. C. (2013). *Multicultural education in a pluralistic society* (9th ed.). Merrill Prentice Hall.
Jian, M., Green, R. J., Henley, T. B., & Masten, W. G. (2009). Acculturation in relation to the acquisition of a second language. *Journal of Multilingual and Multicultural Development, 30*(8), 481–492.
Schumann, J. (1986). Research on the acculturation model for second language acquisition. *Journal of Multilingual and Multicultural Development, 7*(5), 379–392.

Audio-Lingual Method (ALM) is a second language teaching method influenced by behaviorism emphasizing repetition of common phrases to achieve basic oral communication in a relatively short period of time.

ALM emerged pre-WWII during the late 1930s to early 1940s to meet the needs of the military for soldiers to become fluent in the language of their comrades and foes from other countries. The ALM method had its foundation in structural linguistics and focused on aural (listening) and lingual (speaking) aspects of language, marking a shift away from the previous emphasis on reading and writing foreign languages (Saville-Troike, 1973).

Memorization of dialogues and drills on specific language structures dominated ALM as the behaviorist view of learning strongly influenced the field of second language learning at the time (Brown, 2007). Students in ALM classes would be drilled on different phonemes that are similar. Role play and dialogue were featured in this language method. Drills were focused on patterns found in the English language. Often teachers would use a pattern where one word was missing, and students would fill in the blank first with one word and then another appropriate word. For long sentences a backwards buildup drill was utilized, starting with a basic noun phrase, then layering on additional words for a more complex noun phrase. Eventually a verb phrase is added and sometimes an object phrase. The result is a complex lengthy sentence. Often students found this method monotonous and tiresome (Abdel-Rahman, 2009).

While in ALM students learn syntax through repetition, very little time is spent on exploring the meanings of what is being learned. Surface-level learning of the language is accomplished, but deep meaning acquired when students develop the rules for how a language functions is not advanced. Acquiring this deep understanding enables students to create their own sentences and to break the rules, when needed, using poetic license, reflecting a higher level of language competence.

See also: Syntax.

Abu-Melhim, A. R. (2009). Re-evaluating the effectiveness of the audio-lingual method in teaching English to speakers of other languages. *International Forum of Teaching and Studies, 5*(2), 39–45.
Brown, H. D. (2007). *Principles of language learning and teaching* (5th ed.). Pearson.
Saville-Troike, M. (1973). Reading and the audio-lingual method. *TESOL Quarterly, 7*(4), 395–405.

Bilingual Education Act of 1968 is the first piece of federal legislation in the United States that recognized the needs of language minority students and allowed for instruction in students' home language.

The Bilingual Education Act (BEA) came into being as Title VII of the Elementary and Secondary Education Act and was the first comprehensive federal legislation pertaining to the education of language minority students (de Jong, 2013). BEA was first introduced by Senator Ralph Yarbrough in Texas where he attributed the state's high drop-out rate among Mexican-American students to a lack of programs to meet the needs of students learning English as an additional language (Moore, 2021). While some states such as California and Texas already had state and local policies to support language minority students, BEA established the first national policy.

The purpose of BEA was to provide funding for school districts to establish specialized educational programs for students not yet proficient in English. Since education is a state responsibility, the federal government offered financial incentives to school districts in the form of competitive grants to create these programs. The grants were to be used by the districts for: (1) resources for educational programs, (2) training for teachers and teacher aides, (3) development and dissemination of materials, and (4) parent involvement projects. The original version of BEA was ambiguous regarding these parameters and did not explicitly require bilingual instruction or the use of the students' native language for educational purposes.

Since 1968, BEA has been reauthorized numerous times (1974, 1978, 1984, 1988, 1994), each time clarifying the goals and parameters of programs eligible for funding (Wright, 2019). In 2001, however, BEA was replaced with Title III of the No Child Left Behind Act entitled "Language Instruction for Limited English Proficient and Immigrant Students." Notably, the word "bilingual" was omitted from the new legislation and programs employing students' home languages were neither encouraged nor forbidden (Wright, 2019).

See also: Castañeda v. Pickard (1978), Language Policy, Language Planning, Lau v. Nichols (1974), Plyler v. Doe (1982).

de Jong, E. J. (2013). Policy discourses and US language in education policies. *Peabody Journal of Education, 88*(1), 98–111.
Moore, S. C. (2021). *A history of bilingual education in the US: Examining the politics of language policymaking*. Multilingual Matters.
Wright, W. E. (2019). *Foundations for teaching English language learners: Research, theory, policy, and practice* (3rd ed.). Caslon.

Bilingualism (models of) encompasses models that broadly represent different processes of acquiring more than one language.

Subtractive bilingualism entails the weakening of the home language while acquiring an additional language. Early research shows that language minorities usually experience subtractive bilingualism as a result of schooling (Lambert, 1975). Even today, language programs and policies at school that do not support home language development or worse, that penalize use of the home language, contribute to subtractive bilingualism.

Additive bilingualism refers to the process of learning an additional language while continuing to develop the mother tongue. Members of the language majority usually experience additive bilingualism, which involves learning an additional language without jeopardizing the home language. Immersion programs or foreign language programs are considered additive.

Recursive bilingualism encompasses the learning process of reaching back and reaffirming existing heritage language practices to move forward with the language. Recursive bilingualism captures the learning process of individuals, often members of a minoritized group, who are recovering from language loss due to subtractive schooling. These individuals don't begin the process as simple monolinguals, but rather recover and build on existing heritage language practices while further developing in their bilingualism.

Dynamic bilingualism refers to the development of different language practices to varying degrees to interact in increasingly multilingual communities. In this sense, bilingualism is portrayed as adaptive and dynamic and as developing in response to the different purposes for communication that individuals might encounter in different settings. Within this model, the abilities of an individual might vary in one language or another but are nonetheless bilingual because these linguistic practices are adaptive and suit their communicative needs.

See also: Bilinguals (types of), Language Loss, Language Revitalization.

García, O. (2009). *Bilingual education in the 21st century: A global perspective.* John Wiley & Sons.
Lambert, W. E. (1975) *Culture and language as factors in learning and education.* OISE Press.

Bilinguals (types of) are individuals who know more than one language, often to different degrees, and use these languages for a variety of purposes.

Several factors influence bilingual development including the quantity of exposure to each language, quality of input in each language, and the opportunity to use languages across a variety of contexts (Gort, 2019).

Receptive bilinguals are individuals with stronger receptive abilities than productive abilities. In first and second language development, it is commonly observed that receptive language tends to develop prior to the productive skills. Individuals who experience fewer sustained opportunities over time to produce and practice the language are more likely as adults to understand more language than they can express in speech or writing.

Balanced bilinguals are individuals who demonstrate equal levels of ability in two or more languages including across the domains of listening, speaking, reading, and writing. Although this notion of bilingualism is widely accepted, in practice balanced bilingualism is not likely. People who grow up with more than one language can end up being fluent in each language, but there still tends to be a dominant or preferred language for certain settings or tasks.

Sequential bilinguals characterize individuals who start acquiring a new language after they already have a foundation in one language. Individuals who learn an additional language later in life, as early as 3 years of age or even during adulthood, might be considered sequential bilinguals. Sequential bilinguals have the potential to use existing knowledge of a language and language learning strategies to facilitate the learning of the second language.

Simultaneous bilinguals refer to individuals acquiring two languages concurrently from an early age because each parent or caregiver speaks a different language, one language is used at home and a different language outside of the home, or because both parents speak both languages. Even from a young age simultaneous bilinguals can discriminate between and alternate use of the two languages as fitting to the situation.

See also: Bilingualism (models of).

Gort, M. (2019). Developing bilingualism and biliteracy in early and middle childhood. *Language Arts*, 96(4), 229–243.

Castañeda v. Pickard (1981) was tried in the U.S. Fifth Circuit Court and provides guidelines for an ESL or bilingual program to be legally sufficient.

Castañeda v. Pickard provided the parameters for education programs aimed at English learners. It is often referred to as the three-prong test (Drabach & Callahan, 2011). The program must be: (1) based on a sound approach to educating English learners in both the English language and content areas, (2) implemented in a reasonable manner, and (3) monitored for positive results in English language proficiency and content knowledge. This court case, celebrated as a victory for English learners, was instrumental in shaping U.S. Department of Education regulations, mandating compliance for all districts with ESL programs to qualify for federal funding.

Nevertheless, there have been some problems with implementation of the ruling. The first issue is that the case only directly applies to school districts within the then U.S. Fifth Circuit Court of Appeals which in June 1981 included Texas, Louisiana, Mississippi, Alabama, Georgia, and Florida (Coady et al., 2022). However, the U.S. Department of Education's regulations cover all states since each receives a percentage of their funding from the federal government (National Center for Education Statistics, 2022).

Another problem with implementation is the vagueness of the "three prong test" used to determine the adequacy of the program. The first criterion assumes consensus among experts regarding a sound approach to educating English learners. The second criterion assumes the availability of local resources and personnel to carry out the program. The third criterion asks for positive results for English learners yet it is not specified who is responsible for collecting and determining the positivity of these results.

See also: Castañeda v. Pickard (1978), Language Policy, Language Practice, Lau v. Nichols (1974)

Coady, M. R., Ankeny, B., & Ankeny, R. (2022). Is language a 'right' in U.S. education? Unpacking *Castañeda's* reach across federal, state, and district lines. *Language Policy, 21*(3), 305–329.
Drabach, D. B., & Calhoun, R. M. (2011). Right versus reality: The gap between civil rights and English learners' high school educational opportunities. *Teachers College Record, 16558*.
National Center for Education Statistics. (2023). *Public school revenue sources. Condition of education*. U.S. Department of Education, Institute of Education Sciences. https://nces.ed.gov/programs/coe/indicator/cma

Code switching refers to the practice of mixing or changing languages, dialects, or linguistic registers in a single conversation.

Examples of code switching might include conversation where two or more languages or dialects are being used (Myers-Scotton, 2017) or when languages are mixed in advertisements and other environmental print in multilingual environments (Gardner-Chloros, 2009). Early studies focused on the linguistic aspects of code switching including, for example, when, where and with whom Mexican American speakers chose to use Spanish over English, and subsequent studies examined dialect code switching in India, Norway, and other global locations (Nilep, 2006).

In language education research, scholars have not only explored how and why multiple languages are used in the classroom, but also attitudes and policies related to anti-code switching beliefs. Some educators and policymakers believe that languages should be kept separate based on the notion that code switching interferes with learning or on a more nationalistic idea that a national or dominant language must be taught. However, recognizing the advantages of code switching, researchers have sought to encourage rather than restrict the use of multiple languages in the classroom, as it often empowers speakers and enhances their access to content.

More recently, the term translanguaging has emerged as a pedagogical strategy to intentionally embrace the use of multiple language use in the classroom. This term is more expansive and affirming of multilingual communication. Further, unlike code-switching which connotes a speaker going between two distinct, static systems, translanguaging emphasizes that bilinguals flexibly use language across an *integrated system* (Canagarajah, 2011; García & Wei, 2014).

See also: Translanguaging.

Ferguson, G. (2009). What next? Towards an agenda for classroom codeswitching research. *International Journal of Bilingual Education and Bilingualism, 12*(2), 231–241.
García, O., & Wei, L. (2014). *Translanguaging: Language, bilingualism and education.* Palgrave MacMillan.
Gardner-Chloros, P. (2009). *Code-switching.* Cambridge University Press.
Myers-Scotton, C. (2017). *Code-switching. The handbook of sociolinguistics* (pp. 217–237). Oxford University Press.
Nilep, C. (2006). "Code switching" in sociocultural linguistics. *Colorado Research in Linguistics, 19.* https://doi.org/10.25810/hnq4-jv62

Cognates are words in one language that sound or look like words in another language.

Cognates have similar forms and meanings. For example, the word *garage* is a cognate in several languages including Arabic (karaj), Japanese (gareji), Yoruba (gareji), and Russian (garash). Another example is the word *information* with its cognates *información* in Spanish, *informação* in Portuguese, *informazione* in Italian, and *informasjon* in Norwegian. Cognates are due to different languages sharing the same roots such as those originating from Greek or Latin (Freeman & Freeman, 2014).

Not only full words bear similarity but also word parts. For example, a common suffix in English, *-tion* has an equivalent suffix in Spanish, *-ción* and both mean *a state, condition, or process of.* When teaching roots and affixes, it's crucial to help them identify and understand similarities. Encouraging the recognition of first language cognates in a second language is a useful learner strategy (DeCarrico, 2001) and enhances academic vocabulary (Freeman & Freeman, 2014). It's important to clarify that some similar words, like the English word "resume," are not genuine cognates but rather borrowings from another language, in this case from French.

Just as there can be similarities in words between two languages, there are also false cognates or "false friends," which are words that look and/or sound alike across languages but have different meanings. For instance, the Portuguese word 'pretender' may seem similar to the English 'pretend,' but it means 'intend.' Another example is the English 'actually' and the Spanish 'actualmente,' where despite their visual similarity, 'actualmente' means 'currently,' not 'actually.' Such form similarities with differing meanings can pose challenges for second language learners.

Being aware of cognates can facilitate communication. One does not need to know the meanings of all those words to have cognates and false cognates to work in their favor. Asking for clarification when encountering awkward-sounding words can help prevent misunderstandings.

See also: Metalinguistic Awareness, Vocabulary Teaching and Learning

DeCarrico, J. S. (2001). Vocabulary learning and teaching. In M. Celce-Murcia (Ed.), *Teaching English as a second or foreign language* (3rd ed., pp. 285–299). Heinle & Heinle.

Freeman, D. E., & Freeman, Y. S. (2014). *Essential linguistics: What teachers need to know to teach ESL, reading, spelling, grammar* (2nd ed.). Heinemann.

Common European Framework of Reference (CEFR) for Language is a widely used international framework for learning, teaching, and assessment to aid in classifying language ability in any language.

In the early 1990s, the Council of Europe (COE) initiated the development of a standardized leveling system to classify language proficiency. The aim was to promote plurilingualism and help educational institutions and companies recognize the language abilities of linguistically and culturally diverse students and employees. Today the CEFR is used in many places around the world to develop readily recognizable teaching standards and assessments in a variety of languages.

The CEFR is composed of six levels: A1, A2, B1, B2, C1, and C2. The A levels correspond to "beginners or basic users," B levels correspond to "intermediate or independent users," and C levels correspond to "proficient users." The CEFR has become very important in both teaching and learning of a language and its assessment (Heyworth, 2006). Even though the CEFR does not offer or develop specific assessments, its leveling system has been equated to the scales of several well-known standardized language proficiency tests including, for English, the TOEFL, the IELTS, the TOEIC, and others.

The CEFR is used to inform curriculum and syllabus design as well as to the creation of materials and textbooks. Learners themselves reference the CEFR to identify their level of proficiency in a language when applying for a job or when they want to attend a language school. Even ministries and departments of education in several countries have referred to the CEFR (Heyworth, 2006; The CEFR and EF Set, n.d.-a) as a basis for ensuring a certain progression in language learning standards.

Although the CEFR is recognized worldwide, it is important to keep in mind that there are many countries or associations of countries that have their own leveling system based on their own context (The CEFR and EF Set, n.d.-b).

See also: English Language Proficiency (ELP), English Language Proficiency Standards.

Heyworth, F. (2006). The common European framework. *ELT Journal, 60*(2), 181–184.
EF Set. (n.d.-a). *The CEFR & EF set*. https://www.efset.org/cefr/
EF Set. (n.d.-b). *English levels*. https://www.efset.org/cefr/

Common Underlying Proficiency (CPU) refers to the interdependence of concepts, skills, and linguistic knowledge across languages.

Jim Cummins proposed the term Common Underlying Proficiency hypothesizing that a bilingual's two languages are not stored separately in the brain, nor do they compete for dominance. Rather, two or more languages can co-exist and rely on a common underlying language proficiency (Cummins, 1979). To illustrate what this means, Cummins offers the image of a dual iceberg. Above the waterline, separate peaks of the iceberg represent the outwardly distinct features of each language. Beneath the surface, these peaks are represented as joined and emerging from one iceberg. In other words, both languages are outwardly distinct with their unique systems of phonology, morphology, syntax, and lexicon, but are supported by knowledge, experiences, and skills derived from both languages.

Based on the same premise, learners who have developed literacy in one language tend to make better progress in acquiring literacy in the additional language (Cummins, 2000). Subsequent empirical research on children's early literacy offers evidence that literacy development across languages is related (Melby-Lervåg & Lervåg, 2011) but that the potential for direct transfer varies somewhat by skill. For example, phonological awareness, that is, the knowledge that smaller units of sound can be manipulated, is applicable to many languages (Goodrich & Lonigan, 2017). In contrast, print knowledge encompasses language-specific information. For example, the specific letter names and letter-sounds differ across languages, and so should be taught explicitly to multilingual students when learning to read in a new language.

See also: Metalinguistic Awareness, Translanguaging.

Cummins, J. (1979). Linguistic interdependence and the educational development of bilingual children. *Review of Educational Research, 49*(2), 222–251.

Cummins, J. (2000). *Language, power and pedagogy*. Multilingual Matters.

Goodrich, J. M., & Lonigan, C. J. (2017). Language-independent and language-specific aspects of early literacy: An evaluation of the common underlying proficiency model. *Journal of Educational Psychology, 109*(6), 782.

Melby-Lervåg, M., & Lervåg, A. (2011). Cross-linguistic transfer of oral language, decoding, phonological awareness and reading comprehension: A meta-analysis of the correlational evidence. *Journal of Research in Reading, 34*(1), 114–135.

Communicative competence refers to the capacity of learning a language to the point that the learner will know not only grammatical structures and vocabulary, but also language use in context.

Proficiency in a language involves knowing how to use it in different contexts. Knowing what to say, how to say it, to whom, where, and when means knowing how to use language in different social contexts. Communicative competence has become the goal of language teaching (Richards & Rodgers, 2001; Savignon, 2001).

Communicative competence has four dimensions as follows (Canale & Swain, 1980; Canale, 1983):
- Grammatical competence: grammar and vocabulary knowledge, including pronunciation, spelling, and sentence structure.
- Sociolinguistic competence: knowledge of relevant sociocultural relationships or pragmatics.
- Discourse competence: coherence and cohesion, in other words, how the elements of a given interaction are interconnected in relation to each other and its whole.
- Strategic competence: knowing how to use language strategically to establish effective communication, including negotiation of meaning and the ability to balance out what communicators lack.

These competences—grammatical, sociocultural, strategic, and discourse competences—dynamically interact with each other and help form the individual's overall communicative competence (Hymes, 1972).

See also: Communicative Language Teaching (CLT).

Canale, M. (1983). From communicative competence to communicative language pedagogy. In J. C. Richards & R. W. Schmidt (Eds.), *Language and communication* (pp. 2–27). Longman.
Canale, M., & Swain, M. (1980). Theoretical bases of communicative language approaches to second language teaching and testing. *Applied Linguistics, 1*(1), 1–47.
Hymes, D. (1972). On communicative competence. In J. B. Pride & J. Holmes (Eds.), *Sociolinguistics: Selected readings* (pp. 263–269). Penguin.
Richards, J. C., & Rodgers, T. S. (2001). Approaches and methods in language teaching (2nd ed.). Cambridge University Press.
Savignon, S. (2001). Communicative language teaching for the twenty-first century. In M. Celce-Murcia (Ed.), *Teaching English as a second or foreign language* (3rd ed., pp. 13–28). Heinle & Heinle.

Communicative Language Teaching (CLT) is an approach that emphasizes learning and teaching a language for communication.

Communicative Language Teaching emphasizes interaction as the means and goal of learning a language (Savignon, 2001). According to Brown (2007) there are four interconnected characteristics of CLT: (1) classroom goals and activities are focused on developing the ability to communicate, not just grammatical knowledge or knowledge about language; (2) language is presented and used in authentic contexts and for meaningful purposes; (3) fluency and accuracy are both considered important, but maybe be targeted independently at different times in the classroom; (4) students must be prompted to use the language in unrehearsed contexts to be ultimately successful at communication in real contexts outside of the classroom.

Several other teaching approaches and methods have either derived from or employ characteristics of CLT. For example, Content-Based Language Teaching, Task-Based Language Teaching, Whole Language, and Competency-Based Language Teaching all prioritize a learner-centered approach that promotes communication by integrating various language skills through authentic input (Richards & Rodgers, 2001). On the other hand, CLT contrasts with methods emphasizing translation and decontextualized grammar drills such as Direct Translation and Audiolingualism. In communicative classrooms, students will be exposed to activities that promote the negotiation of meaning, language for social interaction, and their abilities to express their needs, interests, and goals (Richards & Rodgers, 2001).

CLT prioritizes learner-centered language experiences. As such, instructors from different traditions often agree on the fundamental role of experience in language acquisition, leading them to embrace CLT and its adaptable versions tailored to students' needs, interests, and goals.

See also: Communicative Competence, Task-Based Language Teaching.

Brown, H. D. (2007). *Principles of language learning and teaching* (5th ed.). Pearson.
Richards, J. C., & Rodgers, T. S. (2001). *Approaches and methods in language teaching* (2nd ed.). Cambridge University Press.
Savignon, S. (2001). Communicative language teaching for the twenty-first century. In M. Celce-Murcia (Ed.), *Teaching English as a second or foreign language* (3rd ed., pp. 13–28). Heinle & Heinle.

Community Language Learning (CLL) is a teaching method that considers the teacher a counselor and each group of students a community where learners will share their emotions first in their first language and then, with the teacher's translation and help, in the target language.

CLL was developed by Charles Curran, who wanted to apply group counseling techniques to second and foreign language learning. CLL is learner-centered and sees the student as a whole-person. Students share their emotional or difficulties such as anxiety, frustration, and embarrassment in relation to language learning in small groups. They do so in their home languages. The teacher, called the *counselor*, will translate what the students have shared, and the students will then say it again in the target language to their classmates, who form a *community* (Samimy & Rardin, 1994).

Given the uncertainty of what students will share exactly, this method regards a textbook as unnecessary because its content may not reflect what learners have to share in order to interact and grow. In a typical CLL lesson students work on translating and reflecting on their feelings in the target language. They also practice transcribing and analyzing their own interactions. Based on how students seem to be using the language, the teacher may decide to design a course of instruction or syllabus based on the grammatical and vocabulary learning needs the students demonstrate.

The criticisms of CLL mostly pertain to the teacher's roles and the course of study. Language teachers are not necessarily trained to be counselors and must be extremely fluent in the students' home languages. In addition, teachers are dependent on the learners' conversations to plan the lessons. This dependency presents some challenges for creating a clear syllabus, learning goals, and assessments from the beginning of instruction.

This approach is most likely to be used with students at beginning levels of the language who are struggling to produce spoken English; the support of small groups and a bi/multilingual teacher creates a supportive learning environment (Bertrand, n.d.).

See also: Affective Filter Hypothesis.

Bertrand, J. (n.d.). *Community language learning*. British Council.
    https://www.teachingenglish.org.uk/article/community-language-learning
Samimy, K. K., & Rardin, J. P. (1994). Adult language learners' reactions to community language learning: A descriptive study. *Foreign Language Annals, 27*(3), 377–390.

Content and Language Integrated Learning (CLIL) is an approach in which an additional language is used for the teaching and learning of content and language (Coyle, 2007).

CLIL is especially popular in places such as Europe, Malaysia, Hong Kong, and other locations where multilingualism is common and where national and school policies encourage the learning of additional languages from a young age (García, 2009). CLIL is like bilingual programs in the United States in the sense that this approach involves content and language integrated learning. However, unlike U.S. bilingual education which is typically offered as a special program and only at some schools, CLIL is a way of teaching languages in mainstream education preschool through secondary education and even vocational education.

CLIL programs tend to include the teaching of the additional language as a subject parallel to the use of the language as a vehicle for content learning. CLIL requires teachers to have high levels of proficiency in the target language and coordination between language-focused teachers and content-focused teachers. This is because the language is used to learn as well as to communicate and because it is the subject matter that terms the language students need to learn. To promote language and content learning, all four language skills are usually combined in a CLIL lesson. Listening and reading activities provide major sources of input. Speaking focuses on fluency rather than accuracy. Finally, writing provides the opportunity to reinforce taught vocabulary and grammatical patterns.

A successful CLIL program or lesson combines elements of the following: content (progression of knowledge, skills, and understanding in relation to specific elements of a defined curriculum), communication (using the language to learn while learning the language), cognition (critical thinking skills), and culture (exposure to a variety of perspectives which deepen awareness of others and self) (Coyle, 2007).

See also: Program Models.

Coyle, D. (2007). Content and language integrated learning: Towards a connected research agenda for CLIL pedagogies. *International Journal of Bilingual Education and Bilingualism*, *10*(5), 543–562.

García, O. (2009). *Bilingual education in the 21st century: A global perspective*. John Wiley & Sons.

Critical Period Hypothesis (CPH) refers to the notion that the ability to acquire a first language is tied directly to age, and that the ideal period to acquire language occurs in the first years of a child's life and plateaus by the time children reach puberty.

In the field of second language acquisition, this idea has been taken up to argue that there is a critical window for acquiring a second language with first language or native-like proficiency (Lenneberg, 1967). Scholars often reason that because first and second language acquisition happen in similar order—that is, certain language structures are learned in a predictable order—that there must be an ideal age range for learning languages. They also claim that brain maturity or "lateralization," the process by which certain parts of the brain are assigned certain functions, also has to do with successful second language acquisition (Brown, 2007). Specifically, individuals are often able to learn to speak without accents before lateralization, suggesting that brain maturity has to do with the acquisition of phonology.

Critics of CPH highlight that age is not always an indicator of successful language acquisition. For example, Snow and Hofnägel's (1978) study of children learning Dutch as an additional language show that older children and youth aged 10–15 acquired Dutch at faster rates than the younger children, suggesting that adolescence, when individuals tend to have formal knowledge of their own language system, can be an optimal time to learn additional languages. Other critics of CPH point out that adults may not be worse at language learning per se, but that the demands on them to command a language are much higher than they are for children. Critics also point out that affective factors are more frequently found with adults than children when learning a language, as adults may feel self-conscious and not wanting to appear incompetent (Freeman & Freeman 2014). While the CPH and the relationship to age and language learning is still debated among scholars, there is strong evidence that adults *and* children can successfully acquire additional languages.

See also: Second Language Acquisition Hypothesis, Stages of Second Language Acquisition.

Brown, D. (2007). *Principles of language learning and teaching* (5th ed.). Pearson.
Freeman, D. E., & Freeman, Y. S. (2014). *Essential linguistics: What teachers need to know to teach ESL, reading, spelling, grammar* (2nd ed.). Heinemann.
Lenneberg, E. (1967). *The biological foundations of language*. Wiley.
Snow, C., & Hoefnagel-Höhle, M. (1978). The critical period for language acquisition: Evidence from second language learning. *Child Development, 49*(4), 1114–1128.

Critical perspectives and pedagogies refer to various approaches that consider how issues and experiences surrounding race, ethnicity, class, sexuality, gender, power, and inequality affect language use, teaching, and learning (Pennycook, 1999).

Critical perspectives and pedagogies are often informed by ideas of social justice in language teaching. These approaches aim to raise awareness of social inequities so that teachers and learners can question unfair power relations in their own lives and be able to advocate ways to change them. Critical approaches have been taken up in several fields including TESOL. According to Pennycook (1999), critical approaches to teaching English have to do with either ensuring marginalized students have access to linguistic resources or by broadening the "mainstream" view of language to make it more inclusive of marginalized voices. Critical approaches encompass a large field of scholarship and teaching methods. A few of the major approaches are outlined below.

Critical pedagogy has its origins in the work of Paolo Friere who taught literacy to illiterate citizens in impoverished regions of Brazil to read for the purpose of questioning and overturning oppression. He believed that teachers have a responsibility to build relationships and work collaboratively with students, rather than to perpetuate authoritarian ways of teaching and knowing (Friere, 1997). These ideas have been taken up in TESOL to center students' lives, experiences, needs, and struggles as the foundation of instruction (Crookes, 2012). Problem Posing is an example of critical pedagogy that can be adapted to language classrooms to help students collaboratively and critically examine problems they have faced and propose solutions for them. Problem posing engages students in critical reflection that promotes English language dialogue and actions for students to advocate for themselves in and out of the classroom (Wallerstein & Auerbach, 2004).

Critical Race Theory (CRT) originated in the field of legal studies in the 1970s to understand how laws and policies are shaped by race (and racism). This theory has been taken up in various fields, including education to analyze the role of racist ideologies in perpetuating inequities between white students and students of color (Ladson-Billings & Tate, 1995). In the field of TESOL, scholars examine how racism permeates systems and individual perceptions, influencing the privileged status of certain language forms and speakers while marginalizing others (Kubota and Lin, 2006). The area of raciolinguistics, which draws from CRT and applied linguistics, considers how racially diverse speakers are often stigmatized or dismissed based on race. Flores and Rosa (2015) critique efforts to hold minoritized speakers (who are often non-white and language learners) to one singular standard of the language based on white, monolingual English. These scholars advocate for the inclusion of multiple forms of language in schools, and, importantly, work to break down hierarchies in how we assign value or status to different forms of languages. Teachers can consider their own instruction in relation to these ideas, and how race-based inequities are perpetuated and may affect their students' experiences in schools and society at large.

Intersectionality grew from CRT to consider how race, ethnicity, gender, language, religion, social class, dis/ability and other facets of identity overlap in the ways individuals, groups, and systems are perceived and treated. The term was coined by legal expert Kimberlé Crenshaw (1989) who noted that gender intertwines in with other identities in important ways (e.g., the experiences and treatment of African American women vary from African American men and also from white women). In line with ideas of intersectionality, scholars such as Motha (2014) argue that teachers in TESOL must understand the history of racism, the colonial expansion of English, and take an international perspective to better understand the intersections of the multiple identities of their multilingual students. Motha and others advocate for pedagogy that helps teachers and learners explore their own intersectional identities and the power relations in their lives, which includes strategies such as examining biases and interviewing and inviting teachers or students to tell stories about their experiences to counter stereotypes and dominant ideas (counter-storytelling).

LatCrit/Asian Crit/TribalCrit are group-specific movements rooted in CRT that have emerged from legal studies to investigate inequities, address discrimination, and advocate for greater inclusion of various marginalized groups. LatCrit and AsianCrit in particular examine immigration policy, language rights, and issues surrounding accent discrimination (Crump, 2014; Delgado Bernal, 2002; Teranishi, 2002). TribalCrit was created to address Native and Indigenous people's experiences with colonization, assimilation, and racism (Brayboy, 2005). These various critical theories have, in turn, influenced the development of LangCrit which looks at how the intersections of identity and language play out in the experiences of language learners (Crump, 2014).

Taken together, these theories and approaches remind educators that classrooms and schools are not neutral spaces. It's important for educators to keep in mind the ways that systemic inequities and power relations can shape a learner's experiences both in and outside the classroom. Teachers can use strategies based in social justice philosophies or culturally responsive or sustaining teaching (Alim & Paris, 2017) to help students not only learn English, but also to develop positive identities and agency as multilingual learners.

See also: Assets-Based Pedagogies.

Brayboy, B. M. J. (2005). Toward a tribal critical race theory in education. *The Urban Review, 37*(5), 425–446.

Crenshaw, K. (1989). Demarginalizing the intersection of race and sex: A black reminist critique of antidiscrimination doctrine, feminist theory and antiracist politics. *University of Chicago Legal Forum, 8*, 139–667.

Crookes, G. (2012). Critical pedagogy in language teaching. *The encyclopedia of applied linguistics*, 1–9.

Crump, A. (2014). Introducing LangCrit: Critical language and race theory. *Critical Inquiry in Language Studies, 11*(3), 207–224.

Delgado Bernal, D. (2002). Critical race theory, Latino critical theory, and critical raced-gendered epistemologies: Recognizing students of color as holders and creators of knowledge. *Qualitative Inquiry, 8*(1), 105–126.

Flores, N., & Rosa, J. (2015). Undoing appropriateness: Raciolinguistic ideologies and language diversity in education. *Harvard Educational Review, 85*(2), 149–171.

Friere, P. (1997). *Pedagogy of the oppressed.* Bloomsbury.

Kayi-Aydar, H., Varghese, M., & Vitanova, G. (2022). Intersectionality for TESOL Education: Connecting theory and justice pedagogy. *CATESOL Journal, 33*, 1.

Kubota, R., & Lin, A. (2006). Race and TESOL: Introduction to concepts and theories. *TESOL Quarterly, 40*(3), 471–493.

Ladson-Billings, G., & Tate, W. F. (1995). Toward a critical race theory of education. *Teachers College Record, 97*(1), 47–68.

Motha, S. (2014). *Race, empire, and English language teaching: Creating responsible and ethical anti-racist practice.* Teachers College Press.

Paris, D., & Alim, H. S. (Eds.). (2017). *Culturally sustaining pedagogies: Teaching and learning for justice in a changing world.* Teachers College Press.

Pennycook, A. (1999). Introduction: Critical approaches to TESOL. *TESOL Quarterly, 33*(3), 329–348.

Sawchuk, S. (2021, May 18). What is critical race theory and why is it under attack. *Education Week.* https://www.edweek.org/leadership/what-is-critical-race-theory-and-why-is-it-under-attack/2021/05

Teranishi, R. (2002). Asian Pacific Americans and critical race theory: An examination of school racial climate. *Equity & Excellence in Education, 35*(2), 144–154.

Wallerstein, N., & Auerbach, E. (2004). *Problem-posing at work: Popular educator's guide.* Grass Roots Press.

Discourse refers to large units, patterns, and styles of language in use.

The term discourse has multiple meanings. In one sense, discourse has been used to refer to linguistic styles or registers of language use, ranging from more or less formal, to very specialized, with certain lexical and grammatical patterns of language use which are used to accomplish particular tasks in particular situations (Malmkjær, 2009). In another sense, discourse is understood as the organization of larger bodies of language, whether oral or written. In this sense, discourse encompasses how coherence, cohesion, and voice are construed over the course of a text, as well as the ultimate style, or genre of the text (narrative, report, explanation, argument, etc.) (Derewianka & Jones, 2016).

In language classrooms, teachers often pay more attention to more fine-grained aspects of language at the word/phrase dimension (for example through vocabulary instruction) or the sentence dimension (by teaching grammar rules). A focus on discourse, on the other hand, requires teachers and students to pay attention to the larger organization, meaning, and feel of a text. The distinction between discourse, sentence, and word-phrase dimensions is helpful for teachers to ensure language patterns are taught over the whole of a text to support students' reading and writing in a wide range of disciplines (Gottlieb & Ernst-Slavit, 2014).

Gee (1990) expands upon the notion of discourse by making a distinction between the linguistic characteristics of discourse, discourse "with a small d," and discourse with a "big D." Discourse "with a big D" considers more than just language and includes how people think, act, interact, and talk in different social situations, doing different activities, and taking on different roles. Hawkins (2004) argues for the importance of valuing different Discourses and helping students to have varied linguistic tool kits so that they can use various Discourses across a variety of settings.

See also: Academic Language, Genre, Systemic Functional Linguistics (SFL).

Derewianka, B., & Jones, P. (2016). *Teaching language in context*. Oxford University Press.
Gee, J. P. (2007). *Social linguistics and literacies: Ideology in discourses*. Routledge.
Gottlieb, M., & Ernst-Slavit, G. (2014). *Academic language in diverse classrooms: Definitions and contexts*. Corwin Press.
Hawkins, M. R. (2004). Researching English language and literacy development in schools. *Educational Researcher, 33*(3), 14–25.
Malmkjær, K. (2009). *The Routledge linguistics encyclopedia*. Routledge.

Disproportionality is a term often used in elementary and secondary education settings to refer to the overrepresentation or underrepresentation of English learners (ELs) in special education (SpEd) programs and services compared with the percentage of their make-up in the larger school population. In other words, if ELs make-up 10% of the total student body, but 40% of all students in SpEd, we would say there is a disproportionate overrepresentation of ELs in SpEd. Disproportionate representation, whether a group is over or underrepresented, can affect the likelihood of referral and the quality of a student's educational experiences.

Data on SpEd enrollment in the U.S. have been recorded since 1968 (Artiles et al., 2010). Overall, ELs are less likely to be identified as a student with a disability than the general student population during the early years of schooling (i.e., grades K-2). However, ELs are overrepresented as having a disability starting in the third grade and up (Samson & Lesaux, 2009). In addition, the percentage of EL students by state who are identified as having a disability is growing rapidly. Between 2012 and 2020 the number of students identified as both ELs and students with disabilities grew by 30% (U.S. Department of Education, 2022).

Using international literature to examine disproportionality with regard to ELs, there is a trend of overrepresentation of ethnic minority students, but not all ethnic minorities. Since many ELs belong to ethnic minorities within their schools, this disproportionality represents many ELs (Cooc & Kiru, 2018). In the Czech Republic, Romani students are overrepresented (Cashman, 2016). Cooper et al. (1991) found higher rates of Afro-Caribbean students identified for special education in England and Wales. In Israel, Palestinian Arab students are identified at a higher rate for disabilities than Jewish students (Kasler & Jabareen, 2017).

When examining possible rationales for this overrepresentation, cultural differences were often cited. Differences between school norms and the cultural practices of minorized communities may underlay the over-identification of disabilities for these groups. Another issue affecting ELs in the United States are exclusionary language policies such as "English Only for Instruction" which by middle school result in poorer academic outcomes for ELs compared to bilingual or dual language instruction (Umansky & Reardon, 2014). These poor academic outcomes often lead to a referral for special education (Gabel et al., 2009).

In the end, it is not the fault of the student group that they are disproportionately represented in the special education disability group. In fact, with ELs, a second or third language is an asset, not a problem. The solution to the disproportionality of ELs within special education is to be found in the school systems and social institutions (Waitoller et al., 2010). Disproportionate representation of ELs in SpEd means a close look at the school's referral and assessment practices are needed, as well as educator knowledge about the academic, linguistic, and cultural backgrounds of ELs, in order to ensure every student receives the optimal programs and services.

See also: U.S. School Procedures for Identification and Services for English Learners.

Artiles, A., Kozleski, E., Trnet, S., Osher, D., & Ortiz, A. (2010). Justifying and explaining disproportionality, 1968–2008: A critique of underlying view of culture. *Exceptional Children, 76*, 279–299.
Cashman, L. (2016). New label no progress: Institutional racism and the persistent segregation of Romani students. *Race Ethnicity and Education, 20*(5), 1–14.
Cooc, N., & Kiru, E. W. (2018) Disproportionality in special education: A synthesis of international research and trends. *The Journal of Special Education, 52*(3), 163–173.
Cooper, P., Upton, G., & Smith, C. (1991). Ethnic minority and ender distribution among staff and pupils in facilities for pupils with emotional and behavioural difficulties in England and Wales. *British Journal of Sociology of Education, 12*, 77–94.
Gabel, S., Curcic, S., Powell, J., Khader, K., & Albee, L. (2009). Migration and ethnic group disproportionality in special education: An exploratory study. *Disability & Society, 24*, 62–639.
Kasler, J., & Jabareen, Y. T. (2017). Triple jeopardy: Special education for Palestinians in Israel. *International Journal of Inclusive Education, 21*, 1261–1275.
Samson, J. F., & Lesaux, N. K. (2009). Language-minority learners in special education: Rates and predictors of identification. *Journal of Learning Disabilities, 42*, 148–162.
Umansky, I., & Reardon, S. (2014). Bilingual, dual immersion, and English immersion classrooms in reclassification patterns among Latino English learner students. *American Educational Research Journal, 51*(5), 879–912.
U.S. Department of Education. (2022). *OSEP fast facts: Students with disabilities who are English Learners (Els) served under IDEA Part B.* Office of Special Education Programs (OSEP). https://sites.ed.gov/idea/osep-fast-facts-students-with-disabilities-english-learners#:~:text=The%20percent%20of%20school%20aged,2012%20to%2011.78%25%20in%202020
Waitoller, F. R., Artiles, A. J., & Cheney, D. A. (2010). The miner's canary: A review of overrepresentation research and explanations. *The Journal of Special Education, 44*, 29–49.

English as a Second Language (ESL) is the widely used abbreviation to refer to learning English as a language additional to one's first or home language.

Terms that are often used interchangeably for ESL include English as a New Language (ENL), English as an Additional Language (EAL), and Teaching English to Speakers of Other Languages (TESOL). However, each term has its own nuance. Many argue that these terms are not neutral and carry certain assumptions and values about the development of one or more languages (Webster & Lu, 2012).

In some U.S. states, instruction geared to teaching English is referred to English as a *new* language to underscore the "newness" of the language regardless of whether students already have a foundation in another language or whether they are learning English with another language simultaneously. The term EAL is often considered assets-based because it emphasizes the student already knows one or more languages and that English is being "added" to the existing language(s). The term TESOL is especially common in adult learning settings or in learning settings where English is not the environmental language.

Sometimes the terms English as a Foreign Language (EFL) and ESL are used interchangeably as if they were synonyms but are in fact not. The environment or setting where English learners learn English is the major difference between ESL and EFL (Anuradha, 2021). Individuals may learn English as a second language to function in a setting where English is used as its official or institutionalized language. Those who learn English as foreign language do not necessarily need English to function where they live, but rather for travel, some internet use, or international communication.

These terms carry over to the names of classes or programs for students learning English, as well as teaching certifications programs or teacher titles and roles. Ultimately, while educators will encounter different terms, the aim is to use the term that is the most accurate and respectful in that setting.

See also: Bilingual (models of), Bilingual (types of), English Learner (EL), L1 and L2.

Anuradha. (2021, November 29). *What is the difference between EFL and ESL?* PEDIAA. https://pediaa.com/what-is-the-difference-between-efl-and-esl/

Webster, N. L., & Lu, C. (2012). "English language learners": An analysis of perplexing ESL-related terminology. *Language and Literacy, 14*(3), 83–94.

English as Lingua Franca (ELF) refers to the linguistic phenomenon wherein English has emerged as the predominant language used globally across diverse contexts and by individuals from various first language backgrounds.

In its role as a lingua franca, English functions as a bridge or vehicular language that facilitates communication in a wide array of settings, often serving as the sole or most effective means of communication (Seidlhofer, 2013). While many individuals learn English with the intent to interact with English-dominant individuals or in English-dominant environments, a significant portion of worldwide English usage transpires among nonnative speakers and outside English-dominant settings (Kachru, 1996).

Many factors have contributed to worldwide spread of the English language starting with colonial rule (Kachru, 1996). English is the most frequently taught foreign language in the world. Research is published more in English than in any other language. The media, including paper publications, radio and TV, records, tapes, and films, are mostly produced in English. English is the official language of international businesses and interactions in conferences, air traffic control, and shipping. Paper and electronic mail predominantly occur in the English language as well as interactions and publications on the internet (Alatis, 2005).

An important point of consideration is the cultural dimension of ELF. While some perceive a lingua franca as culturally neutral (House, 2003), others argue that ELF is inherently multicultural. This perspective contends that ELF users bring their unique cultural identities into their language usage, thereby influencing their linguistic performances (Pölzl & Seidlhofer, 2006).

See also: Native speaker (NS) and Nonnative Speaker (NNS), World Englishes.

Alatis, J. E. (2005). Kachru's circles and the growth of professionalism in TESOL. *English Today*, 82(21), 25–34.
House, J. (2003). English as a lingua franca: A threat to multilingualism? *Journal of Sociolinguistics*, 7(4), 556–578.
Kachru, B. B. (1996). World Englishes: Agony and ecstasy. *The Journal of Aesthetic Education*, 30(2), 135–155.
Martin-Rubió, X. (2018). *Contextualising English as a lingua franca: From data to insights*. Cambridge Scholars Publishing.
Pölzl, U., & Seidlhofer, B. (2006). In and on their own terms: The 'habitat factor' in English as a lingua franca interactions. *International Journal of the Sociology of Language*, 177, 151–176.
Seidlhofer, B. (2013). *Understanding English as a lingua franca*. Oxford University Press.

English for Specific Purposes (ESP) refers to instruction mainly intended for intermediate and advanced adults learning English for a specific purpose.

Specific purposes for learning the language are often related to academic and professional pursuits including English for business; English for science; and English for pilots (Johns & Dudley-Evans, 1991). A further subgroup is English for Academic Purposes (EAP). Under this umbrella, some examples of EAP would be English for Science and Technology, English for Business and Economics, English for Medical Purposes, and English for the Law. Like any ESP course, one of the challenges in EAP is to find teachers that have the language teaching and the specific content knowledge to teach the courses.

ESP emphasizes ways in which language is used in real communication. ESP aims to meet the specific learning needs of language learners, given where they work, learn, and how they use English. In a typical ESP course, the instructor considers the following: a needs assessment, discourse analysis or an in-depth study of the language used in the specific field, and development of course materials (Johns & Dudley Evans, 1991). This helps ensure that the course addresses the learners' specific purposes for learning the language.

Many argue the ESP can play a vital role in "equipping students with the communicative skills to participate in specific academic and professional cultural contexts" (Hyland, 2002, p. 394). However, there are also critiques. One critique stems from a larger global criticism that English has been determined to be the lingua franca in high status fields, such as science and technology, which unfairly requires people in these positions to learn the language required to be conversant in this field (Basturkmen, 2014). Others argue that English classes that focus broadly on the rules of speech (rhetoric) and literacy can provide an adequate knowledge base to be translatable to any discipline (Johns & Dudley-Evans, 1991; Hyland, 2002).

See also: Intensive English Program (IEP).

Basturkmen, H. (2014). *Ideas and options in English for specific purposes*. Routledge.
Hyland, K. (2002). Specificity revisited: How far should we go now? *English for Specific Purposes, 21*(4), 385–395.
Johns, A. M., & Dudley-Evans, T. (1991). English for specific purposes: International in scope, specific in purpose. *TESOL Quarterly 25*(2), 297–314.

THE LANGUAGE OF TESOL AND BILINGUAL EDUCATION

English Language Proficiency (ELP) refers to the continuum of language development from a very beginning level of skill in the language to a very capable degree of skill in the language.

A variety of factors influence a learner's level of ELP at any point in time, including years of exposure to English, years of access to quality instruction in the English language, and whether English is used in the home along with another language, etc.

For assessment purposes, ELP is often divided into 5 levels beginning with Level 1 through Level 5. Depending on the assessment used to determine a student's ELP level, the term referring to a student's linguistic proficiency at each level varies, yet the system of levels is quite similar as illustrated in the chart below with commonly used ELP assessment instruments and levels in the U.S. Most ELP assessments score students in each of the four domains of language—reading, writing, listening and speaking. Together these domain scores make up a composite score, that the ELP level is based on.

Instrument	Level 1	Level 2	Level 3	Level 4	Level 5
Arizona English Language Learning Assessment (AZELLA)	Pre-emergent	Emergent	Basic	Low intermediate	High intermediate
English Language Proficiency Assessment for the 21st century (ELPA 21)	Beginning	Early intermediate	Intermediate	Early advanced	Advanced
English Language Proficiency Assessment for California (ELPAC)	Entering		Expanding		Bridging
New York State English as a Second Language Achievement Test (NYSESLAT)	Entering	Emerging	Transitioning	Expanding	Commanding
Texas English Language Proficiency Assessment System (TELPAS)	Beginning		Intermediate	Advanced	Advanced high
WIDA Access for ELLS	Entering	Emerging	Developing	Expanding	Bridging (Level 6 Reaching)

It is important to note that the ELP assessments listed here are annual summative assessments, meaning they provide a snapshot of students' ELP at a given time. ELP Assessment data is often used for school accountability purposes, that is, to monitor the progress of students identified as English learners and accordingly make decisions about programs, services, and hiring (Wright, 2019). It is also important to note that teachers might use classroom assessments to gauge progress with ELP on a more fine-grained level and thereby adjust instruction accordingly.

The Test of English as a Foreign Language (TOEFL) is an internationally recognized standardized test to assess the ELP of adults. It is commonly used for admission to English-speaking universities and for visa or immigration purposes. The TOEFL has five levels for speaking and writing and four levels for reading and listening. In comparison to the ELP assessments used at elementary and secondary grades, the TOEFL has Level 1 as the highest level instead of the lowest level. The International English Language Testing System (IELTS) has the same purpose as the TOEFL, but based in the United Kingdom, is often more commonly used for admission to English-speaking universities outside of the United States. The IELTS has 9 levels ranging from ("did not attempt the test" to "expert user"). Teachers of adult learners planning to take these tests should understand the specific language proficiency requirements of their students' target institutions, provide tailored test preparation, monitor progress, and offer guidance on resources and strategies to help students succeed in TOEFL and IELTS exams for academic and immigration purposes.

See also: Common European Framework of Reference (CEFR) for Language, English Language Proficiency Standards, U.S. School Procedures for Identification and Services for English Learners.

Herrera, S. G., Murry, K. G., & Cabral, R. M. (2020). *Assessment of culturally and linguistically diverse students* (3rd ed.). Pearson.

Wright, W. E. (2019). *Foundations for teaching English language learners: Research, theory, policy, and practice* (3rd ed.). Caslon.

English Language Proficiency Standards are guidelines that specify the language skills and proficiency levels for assessing and instructing students learning English as an additional language at school.

English Language Proficiency (ELP) Standards serve as benchmarks for assessing and improving the language skills of students identified as English learners (ELs). These standards provide a framework to guide educators, policymakers, and curriculum developers in fostering effective English language development and equitable educational opportunities for ELs.

In the United States, ELP Standards are informed by the expertise of organizations like WIDA and ELPA 21, as well as state-specific entities. The WIDA ELP Standards are broadly organized by content area, common purposes for language use, mode of communication, and grade level (WIDA, 2020). ELPA 21 organizes its ELP standards along receptive and productive skills with correspondences to content areas and grade-appropriate tasks (ELPA 21, 2021). Other states develop and use their own English Language Proficiency Standards including Arizona, California, Texas, and others.

As part of a high-stakes accountability system, some common critiques of English Language Proficiency Standards include concerns about their potential to promote a narrow focus on discrete language skills, an overemphasis on standardized testing at the expense of meaningful communication, and a lack of flexibility to accommodate the diverse needs and backgrounds of English learners (Solórzano, 2008). Nonetheless, educators should be familiar with students' English proficiency levels to tailor instruction, integrate language objectives into lesson plans, and provide appropriate scaffolding. Collaborating with specialists and families is also important to monitor progress.

See also: English Language Proficiency Standards, English Learner, U.S. School Procedures for Identification and Services for English Learners.

ELPA21. (2021). *Understanding ELPA21 student reports: A quick guide for educators. English Language Proficiency Assessment for the 21st Century (ELPA21)*. https://www.education.ne.gov/wp-content/uploads/2021/12/ELPA21-Quick-Guide-to-Understanding-Reports.pdf

Solórzano, R. W. (2008). High stakes testing: Issues, implications, and remedies for English language learners. *Review of Educational Research, 78*(2), 260–329.

WIDA. (2020). *WIDA English language development standards framework, 2020 edition: Kindergarten–grade 12*. Board of Regents of the University of Wisconsin System.

English Learner (ELS) is a commonly used term to refer to students learning English in school settings and whose primary language is a language other than English.

Terms for ELs that are often interchangeably used include Culturally and Linguistically Diverse (CLD) learners, Emergent Bilinguals (EBs), Dual Language Learners (DLL), and Multilingual Learners (ML). While these terms are used in reference to roughly the same group of students, each term highlights a certain aspect of the learner. EL is a legal- and policy-oriented term referring to students who by federal law are eligible to receive English language development services (Linquanti & Cook, 2013). The term CLD learner focuses on the uniqueness of students' background (Bardack, 2010) and can refer to students of varying linguistic and cultural backgrounds, not solely those who qualify for English language services. The term EB is often used as a more assets-based term than EL because it emphasizes a student's bilingualism (García, 2009). DLL is similar with its assets-based orientation and is often used in reference to young learners who are learning both languages simultaneously from an early age. Lastly, the term MLs is similarly an assets-focused term in that draws attention to children's and adults' abilities in multiple languages and dialects.

The use of these terms is often shifting and dynamic. Many times, educators use the terms prevalent in their school or language center. Nonetheless terms suggest a certain attitude or stance to these students and their language development. Using asset-based terms has the potential to change the perception of these students among policymakers, educators, family members, and importantly among students themselves (García, 2009).

See also: Bilinguals (types of), U.S. School Procedures for Identification and Services for English Learners.

Bardack, S. (2010). *Common ELL terms and definitions.* American Institutes for Research. https://www.air.org/sites/default/files/downloads/report/NEW_-_Common_ELL_TERMS_AND_DEFINITIONS_6_22_10_0.pdf

García, O. (2009). Emergent bilinguals and TESOL: What's in a name? *TESOL Quarterly, 43*(2), 322–326.

Linquanti, R., & Cook, H. G. (2013). Toward a "common definition of English learner": Guidance for states and state assessment Consortia in defining and addressing policy and technical issues and options. *Council of Chief State School Officers.* https://files.eric.ed.gov/fulltext/ED565753.pdf

Error correction refers to how errors are corrected or how more competent users of a language (usually the teacher) give feedback so that the student can correct the error.

Error correction is an issue in second language acquisition research and practice that has been studied for some time. For example, Hendrickson (1978) investigated issues such as, should learners be corrected? When? Which errors require correction? And who should do the correcting? Generally, a language learner will make a variety of grammatical or pronunciation errors in their spoken language and grammatical or spelling errors in written language. Errors are often a sign of learning and progress with a language. For example, a speaker who has learned past tense, may added to every verb and disregard irregular verbs (like run/ran or teach/taught). These kinds of errors show the learner attempting to generalize a rule, and therefore, they are making progress with the language (Lightbown & Spada, 2013).

Because spoken errors come in many forms and are often a sign of progress in second language acquisition, researchers do not agree on a single, optimal way to correct errors. However, researchers have looked at the various forms of error correction and make some preliminary recommendations (Lyster & Ranta, 1997).

Explicit correction involves providing the correct form of the language to the speaker.

St: I runned to the park.
T: You mean *ran*.

Recast is when the teacher repeats back what the student has said but provides a corrected form in their utterance.

St: I runned to the park.
T: I ran to the park.

Clarification request occurs when a teacher does not correct the error but instead asks the student to clarify.

St: I runned to the park.
T: Pardon me?

Metalinguistic feedback is a form of feedback that points out that there is an error but requires the learner to isolate and correct it.

St: I runned to the park.
T: There's an error in that verb. What is it?

Elicitation involves repeating the speaker's sentence and asking them to fill in the blank of where the error occurs:

St: I runned to the park.
T: I ____ to the park?

Repetition is when the error is simply repeated for the learner to correct.

St: I runned to the park.
T: Runned?

Evidence of successful error correction may be seen when the student is able to correct the error and then learn from it, so that they can correct future mistakes. Research suggests that allowing students to correct their own errors is more effective than explicit correction or recasting because learners can work on finding and learning correct forms of language themselves (Lyster & Ranta, 1997).

Another aspect of error correction occurs in writing. While there is little consensus on the ideal way to provide feedback, researchers concur that having opportunities to revise written work is essential so that students can integrate feedback in meaningful ways into their writing (Polio, 2012).

To conclude, errors are a common and even welcome sign of second language acquisition. Teachers have many choices for providing corrective feedback. Teachers can keep in mind whether the error correction would be beneficial or, on the other hand, impede the flow of communication. If so, teachers could always take note of common errors among students and address these during class in a way that doesn't put the learner on the spot.

See also: Fossilization.

Hendrickson, J. M. (1978). Error correction in foreign language teaching: Recent theory, research, and practice. *The Modern Language Journal*, 62(8), 387–398.
Lightbown, P., & Spada, N. M. (2013). *How languages are learned* (4th ed.). Oxford University Press.
Lyster, R., & Ranta, L. (1997). Corrective feedback and learner uptake: Negotiation of form in communicative classrooms. *Studies in Second Language Acquisition*, 19(1), 37–66.
Polio, C. (2012). The relevance of second language acquisition theory to the written error correction debate. *Journal of Second Language Writing*, 21(4), 375–389.

Figurative Language, while often challenging for those new to learning the English language, aids in creative discourse and expands the English learner's expressive language.

Figurative language includes idioms and metaphors. It is important for English learners (ELs) to be provided with scaffolded exposure to help them understand and express themselves using figurative language (Palmer et al., 2007). While similes compare two things that may seem dissimilar at first glance, the word *like* or *as* signals that it is a figure of speech such as in the sentence "The agile boxer moves *as light as a feather*." Explicit discussion helps ELs know it is not meant literally. However, idioms and metaphors, on the other hand, do not make use of indicator words which may lead ELs to interpret these meanings literally.

Idioms (or idiomatic expressions) are expressions used to describe a situation or action where the intended meaning is different from the literal meaning. Idiomatic expressions are used to describe a situation or action such as in "That homework assignment was a 'piece of cake'." This can be confusing for ELs who often rely on the literal meanings of words and find that the sentence or message overall don't make sense (Al-Khawaldeh et al., 2016). The good news is that idioms are found in a wide range of languages and cultures so students from different backgrounds can relate to English idioms by sharing idioms from their home languages.

Metaphors, like idiomatic expressions, don't rely on signals such *like* or *as* to compare one thing to another. For example, imagine someone saying, 'Her laughter is a bubbling brook.' In this metaphor, the person's laughter is compared to the sound and liveliness of a bubbling brook. It suggests that her laughter is joyful and refreshing, just like the sounds of a natural stream. Like idioms, metaphors add depth and richness to language but cannot be taken literally.

See also: Academic Language.

Al-Khawaldeh, N., Jaradat, A., Al-momani, H., Baker, B.-K. (2016). Figurative idiomatic language: Strategies and difficulties of understanding English idioms. *International Journal of Applied Linguistics & English Literature, 5*(6), 119–133.

Palmer, B. C., Shackelford, V. S., Miller, S. C., & Leclere, J. T. (2007). Bridging two worlds: Reading comprehension, figurative language instruction, and the English-language learner. *Journal of Adolescent & Adult Literacy, 50*(4), 258–267.

Fossilization refers to errors that persist in advanced second language learner speech, despite education and error correction.

Errors that might persist include the use or omission of articles (the and a) or pronunciation errors. A key idea found in Selinker's (1972) theory is that learners will reach a point in their language learning when errors become so ingrained, they are "fossilized" in their development of a second language, that is, each learner will eventually hit a ceiling in their learning where they will continue to make errors that will impede their goal of speaking fluently and error free in the language. In other words, language development will always stop short of the learner's goal (Tarone, 2012).

Although fossilization is a well-accepted concept, Han (2004) points out that the term is often overly applied to many issues language learners face like backsliding in language learning, making persistent errors, or generally reaching a plateau in a second language learning. It has been attributed to such issues as learner indifference or dissatisfaction with instruction. Han argues that it is important for teachers to know about fossilization in order to find strategies to engage learners and teach difficult concepts in English.

An error that has become a habit and used subconsciously can be difficult to change. Teachers can help learners identify the error type they are making as well as the cause of the error (for example, does the error come from the speaker's first language? Is it an overgeneralization of a rule?). Teachers can also show the student how the correct pattern works in English. However, when engaged in spontaneous speech, the incorrectly developed habit may reemerge. Teachers must consider how much direct instruction to put into addressing fossilized habits and help students continue developing in other areas of their second language, even if it means accepting certain errors (Brown, 2007).

See also: Error Correction, Interlanguage.

Brown, H. D. (2007). *Principles of language learning and teaching* (5th ed.). Pearson.
Han, Z. (2004). Fossilization: Five central issues. *International Journal of Applied Linguistics, 14*(2), 212–242.
Selinker, L. (1972). Interlanguage. *International Review of Applied Linguistics, 10*, 209–231.
Tarone, E. (2012). Interlanguage. *The encyclopedia of applied linguistics* (pp. 1–7). Wiley Blackwell.

Genre refers to distinctive ways of organizing language to communicate for different purposes.

Genre is defined as the organization of language choices to achieve a particular communicative purpose. In the field of linguistics, genres can be written, oral, or involve multiple modes (e.g., written text with visuals or oral text with gestures). For example, business reports, news broadcasts, speeches, letters, and recipes, would also be considered genres because they serve a specific function and make use of certain kinds of language in very specific contexts.

In educational settings, researchers have identified and discussed common genres at school (Brisk, 2014). These genres are often linked to the different content areas (e.g., report, narrative, argument, etc.). For example, explanations are used to explain how something works or why something happens. They involve reasoning and language that demonstrates the understanding of cause and effect. The genre of explanation is commonly used when students show mathematical reasoning, link historical events, and explain scientific phenomena.

Genre-based pedagogy is an approach that centers genre in reading and writing instruction (Rose & Martin, 2012). Proponents of genre-based pedagogy assert that familiarizing students with the purpose and organization of high-leverage genres can help students, particularly multilingual learners, better navigate, comprehend, and produce school-based texts (Brisk, 2014) and critically analyze language in out-of-school contexts (Harmann, 2018). Whether teachers adopt a genre-based pedagogy or not, it is helpful to be observant of the different genres of language in school-based reading, writing and communication.

See also: Discourse, Systemic Functional Linguistics (SFL)

Brisk, M. E. (2014). *Engaging students in academic literacies: Genre-based pedagogy for K-5 classrooms*. Routledge.
Derewianka, B., & Jones, P. (2016). *Teaching language in context*. Oxford University Press.
Harman, R. (Ed.). (2018). *Bilingual learners and social equity: Critical approaches to systemic functional linguistics*. Springer.
Rose, D., & Martin, J. R. (2012). *Learning to write, reading to learn: Genre, knowledge and pedagogy in the Sydney school*. Equinox.

Grammar Translation Method (GTM) of teaching a second language emphasizes grammar and translation with minimal regard for phonology since this method was primarily used for learning written language and not oral communication.

GTM was common since the 1800s and is still used today. It started as a method for teaching Latin which has no communicative component since it was no longer a spoken language. While this method lacks a theory base, its survival as a method for teaching language seems to owe its continuation to teachers teaching the way they have been taught. This method is heavy on one-way teacher transmission of knowledge and tends to be less interactive for students than communicative methods (Natsir & Sanjaya, 2014). From a students' viewpoint there is a great deal of time spent memorizing verb conjugations and grammar rules pertaining to the target language. After learning the rules, students are required to then translate from their native language to the target language. Hence, in this method there was a heavy emphasis on learning words and word parts (morphology) and no need for learning the sound system (phonology). Eventually researchers questioned why a method used to teach an unspoken language was being used for modern language teaching and other methods emerged (Wright, 2015).

While this method has its limitations as it doesn't address phonology, it finds application in certain educational contexts. In Jordan this method is viewed as especially useful when there are grammatical forms in the target language students are having difficulty with (Aqel, 2013). A study by Assalahi (2013) revealed that Arab English as a Foreign Language (EFL) teachers, even though trained in communicative language teaching, predominantly employed the grammar translation model due to their forms-focused perspective. This preference seems to stem from their exposure to this method during university training and preparation.

See also: Morphology.

Aqel, I. M. (2013). The effect of using grammar-translation method on acquiring English as a foreign language. *International Journal of Asian Social Science, 3*(12), 2469–2476.

Assalahi, H. M. (2013) Why is the grammar-translation method still alive in the Arab world? Teachers' beliefs and its implications for EFT teacher education. *Theory and Practice in Language Studies, 3*(4), 589–599.

Natsir, M., & Sanjaya, D. (2014). Grammar Translation Method (GTM) versus Communicative Language Teaching (CLT): A review of literature. *International journal of Education & Literacy Studies, 2*(1), 58–62.

Wright, W. E. (2015). *Foundations for teaching English language learners: Research, theory, policy and practice* (2nd ed.). Caslon.

Heritage Language Learners is used in reference to individuals with a connection to an ancestral language.

The term heritage language learner emphasizes a personal or historical connection to an ancestral language regardless of language ability, degree of exposure, or school-based learning (Valdés, 2001). Heritage language programs are intended for heritage language learners, rather than individuals from outside a given community. Historically, language minoritized communities have promoted heritage language learning through, for example, community-based after-school or weekend programs often held at community centers or churches (Wiley & Valdés, 2000). Today, heritage language programs can be found in conventional school-based K-12 bilingual education and foreign language programs; Native or indigenous language and culture education in tribal colleges, mentor-apprentice partnerships, immersion camps, early childhood programs; or college-level courses for second or third-generation immigrant students studying their heritage language as a foreign language (Hornberger & Wang, 2017).

One of the biggest challenges to establishing heritage language programs is teacher proficiency in the target language. In the United States, only 10% of Native American/Alaska Indian students in grades 4 and 8 have teachers with heritage language speaking capability (Office of English Language Acquisition, 2022). However, promising strategies include culturally responsive instruction, biliteracy development, family and community engagement, and teacher training and professional development (Office of English Language Acquisition, 2022).

See also: Bilinguals (models of), English Learner, L1 and L2, Language Loss, Language Revitalization, Native American Languages Act

Hornberger, N. H., & Wang, S. C. (2017). Who are our heritage language learners?: Identity and biliteracy in heritage language education in the United States. In *Heritage language education* (pp. 3–36). Routledge.

Office of English Language Acquisition. (2022). *Heritage language learners and American Indian and Alaska native students*. https://ncela.ed.gov/files/fast_facts/HeritageLanguageInfographic_FINAL_508.pdf

Valdés, G. (2001). Heritage language students: Profiles and possibilities. In J. K. Peyton, D. A. Ranard, & S. McGinnis (Eds.), *Heritage languages in America: Preserving a national resource* (pp. 37–77). Center for Applied Linguistics and Delta Systems.

Wiley, T. G., & Valdés, G. (2000). Editors' introduction: Heritage language instruction in the United States: A time for renewal. *Bilingual Research Journal, 24*(4), III–VII.

Homonyms in the narrowest sense are words that sound the same and look the same—"lean" as in "the lean steak had little fat" and "lean" as in "he leaned on his cane." However, the definition of homonyms has loosened to include words that sound the same but have different spellings and/or meanings which is the same definition used for "homophone." For example, "rein" and "rain" sound the same, are spelled differently, and have different meanings. They are homonyms and also homophones.

Homographs are spelled the same but have different pronunciation and/or different meanings. "Bat" as in the small flying animal and "bat" meaning a wooden stick in, sound the same and are spelled the same, but have different meanings. So, they are an example of a homonym, homophone and homograph. The bow on top of a gift and the bow of a ship are homographs since they are spelled the same but are pronounced differently and have different meanings. Some would call them homonyms since they are spelled the same. As Manedova (2019) noted, there is not a generally accepted definition of homonyms.

Heteronyms where the spelling is the same as a homograph, but the pronunciation and meaning are different can also be challenging. An example here would be "desert" a very dry region and "desert" meaning to leave. To make it more complicated, the second "desert" is pronounced the same as "dessert" such as cake or cookies and the last two are homophones.

As teachers, it is helpful to anticipate what is likely to cause confusion to English learners. In conversation, homophones would be the most confusing and in reading homographs. Certain books can be read as a humorous way to introduce homonyms such as *The King Who Rained* and *Chocolate Moose for Dinner* (Freeman & Freeman, 2014).

See also: Orthography.

	Same pronunciation	Different pronunciation
Same spelling	■▲●	●◻
Different spelling	■▲	

■ Homonym, ▲ Homophone, ● Homograph, ◻ Heteronym/heterophone.

Freeman, D. E., & Freeman, Y. S. (2014). *Essential linguistics: What teachers need to know to teach esl, reading, spelling, grammar* (2nd ed.). Heinemann.
Mamedova, M. (2019). Classification of homonyms of the English language. *European Journal of Research and Reflection in Educational Sciences, 7*(12), 1–5.

Individual learner differences refer to the researched differences among language learners when they are developing an additional language.

Several bodies of research aim to account for or even predict a person's success at learning a language, recognizing that not everyone achieves the same desired level of proficiency. This research broadly explores factors contributing to variation in language learning success. Key considerations include age, motivation, and personality (Lightbown & Spada, 2013), as well as environmental factors related to language learning (Norton & Toohey 2000).

Age
Under most circumstances, since individuals learn a first language during childhood with ease, second language researchers have investigated the role that age plays in learning. The so-called Critical Period Hypothesis posits that there is a window during which second language learning is optimal, namely, before adolescence (Lennenberg, 1967). Research looking at age often examines the role of age and pronunciation, learning of grammar, and rate of learning (Lightbown & Spada, 2013). While it does appear that younger learners do learn differently and have advantages in learning pronunciation, older learners bring other strengths to language learning. Among these strengths are a metalinguistic awareness of grammar, vocabulary, and often motivation and goals related to communication. In this sense, age does to some degree explain differences in acquiring a second language.

Motivation and Personality
Individual characteristics related to motivation and personality type and their relationship to language learning have also been investigated. Scholars focusing on motivation examine such issues as learners' attitudes, feelings about the language or interest in language, desire to learn (Masgoret & Gardner, 2003), or even the systems of thinking that guide a language learner as they envision their future selves as proficient in the target language (Ushioda & Dörnyei, 2009). In addition to motivation, scholars look at such factors as learning styles or personality types as they are related to the outcomes of learning a language. Factors such as inhibition versus risk taking, introversion versus extroversion, or even a learner's level of anxiety can play a role (Lightbown & Spada, 2013).

Environmental Factors
Another group of scholars reject the idea that language learning can be attributed to psychological concepts like motivation and personality. Instead, these scholars propose that concepts like personality and motivation are not

fixed constructs that reside in everyone, but rather are better understood as products of the social environment (Norton & Toohey, 2000). They describe how forces like discrimination in classrooms and society can greatly influence a learner's experience and success (Norton & Toohey, 2000). Similarly, the social and affective environment of the classroom or broader society where students live can also have an influence on a student's learning outcomes.

While each of these areas of study have made substantive contributions to how we understand the variables that affect second language acquisition, there is no consensus about one singular factor that makes a language learner successful in acquiring an additional language. It is important to create environments that are responsive to individual differences and celebratory of cultural assets to set up learners so that they can have the most agency and success in their learning as possible.

See also: Assets-Based Pedagogies, Critical Period Hypothesis

Lightbown, P., & Spada, N. M. (2013). *How languages are learned* (4th ed.). Oxford University Press.

Masgoret, A. M., & Gardner, R. C. (2003). Attitudes, motivation, and second language learning: A meta-analysis of studies conducted by Gardner and associates. *Language Learning, 53*(S1), 167–210.

Norton, B., & Toohey, K. (2011). Identity, language learning, and social change. *Language Teaching, 44*(4), 412–446.

Ushioda, E., & Dörnyei, Z. (2009). *Motivation, language identities and the L2 self: A theoretical overview.* Multilingual Matters.

Input Hypothesis states that people acquire language through comprehensible input whether oral or written.

Krashen, who originally proposed this hypothesis, named it the Input Hypothesis, but later rebranded it as the Comprehension Hypothesis to emphasize that the input must be comprehensible or should be one level above the student's current comprehension. Also known as i+1, this hypothesis encourages teachers to teach one level above the student's current comprehension (Krashen, 1982). This corresponds to the practice of using reading materials one level above the student's independent reading level for instruction.

Krashen views language production as a result of acquisition and not something that is taught. In addition, according to his theory, grammar does not need to be explicitly taught. Students who are given enough comprehensible input at the level just above the one they are currently at will start using correct grammatical structures on their own (Gass & Selinker, 2001).

Teachers adjust their own speech or provide carefully selected reading samples as well as additional contextual clues to make instruction comprehensible to students. For oral vocabulary teachers speaking slowly, articulating clearly, and letting students see their mouth movements may be helpful. For written language, photos, pictorial representations, anchor charts, cognates, and graphic organizers can make the input comprehensible to students (Levine & McCloskey, 2013).

While Krashen's theory has a large group of proponents, classroom teachers decry the lack of direct instruction in grammar and other aspects of language. Some research points out that there is only so much of a second language can be acquired without direct instruction (Lightbown & Spada, 2013).

See also: Acquisition Theory, Affective Filter Hypothesis.

Gass, S. M., & Selinker, L. (2001). *Second language acquisition: An introductory course* (2nd ed.). Earlbaum Associates.
Krashen, S. D. (1982). *Principles and practice in second language acquisition.* Pergamon Press.
Levine, L. N., & McCloskey, M. L. (2013). *Teaching English language and content in mainstream classes: One class, many paths* (2nd ed.). Pearson.
Lightbown, P. M., & Spada, N. (2013). *How languages are learned* (4th ed.). Oxford University Press.

Intensive English Programs (IEPs) specialize in preparing post-secondary students to attend university programs that use English as the medium of instruction.

IEPs are often post-secondary, pre-academic programs whose classes are non-credit (Thompson, 2013). IEPs mostly enroll international students who have finished high school, bachelor's, or master's degrees in their home countries and who are honing their academic English skills in preparation to pursue an academic degree in an English-speaking country (Richards & Schmidt, 2010).

IEPs can be university affiliates or part of a university department. IEPs can also be private schools that are not directly related to a university. There are also IEPs in countries such as China and Japan, where English is not an official or institutionalized language but where there is growing interest in preparing to study abroad (Li & Xie Fincham, 2018).

As the name implies, IEPs are intensive programs, so students might take as many as 20 or more hours of instruction per week. In addition to survival and academic English, IEPs prepare students to succeed in mainstream university classes and in the new community where they live by providing orientation on intercultural competence and common expectations in academia. Many times, IEP courses are leveled to help ensure students reach their language goals or courses are specific to developing the language domains, for example, academic reading and writing. After attending IEPs programs, international students are well-positioned to continue their academic trajectories in either undergraduate or graduate programs.

Note, it is important not to confuse the abbreviation for Intensive English Program (IEP) with the Individualized Educational Program or Plan (IEP) offered in American public schools to children who have special needs and qualify to receive specialized services.

See also: Language Domains, English for Specific Purposes (EPS).

Li, G., & Xie Fincham, N. (2018). Intensive English language programs. In J. I. Liontas (Ed.), *The TESOL encyclopedia of language teaching.* John Wiley & Sons.

Richards, J. C., & Schmidt, R. (2010). *The Longman dictionary of language teaching & applied linguistics* (4th ed.). Pearson.

Thompson, A. (2013). Intensive English programs in the United States: An overview of structure and mentoring. *TESOL Journal, 4*(2), 211–232.

Interlanguage refers to the emergent linguistic system a learner develops and references while learning a new language.

Selinker (2014) refers to interlanguage as the "linguistic cognitive space that exists between the native language and the language that one is learning" (p. 223). This notion is based on the observation that language learners produce language (often with errors) that is neither solely related to their first language nor the target language. Under this theory, there is not only an innate biological mechanism for learning language (Universal Grammar), but also a "learning language" that learners draw from that is unique from the first language and the target language. This theory stems from the idea that there is a Universal Grammar, an innate, biological system that facilitates language learning. Eventually through, through a variety of opportunities to interact, learners sort out the ways that the target language is used and gradually achieve proficiency. This theory is unique because it means that language learners aren't referring back to their first language or other acquired language, but instead that they are drawing from accumulated linguistic knowledge influenced by the target language, native language, and other languages acquired by the learner (Tarone, 2012). For example, a Tagalog speaker who is learning English may be activating prior language from their first language, other languages they have learned, and a general metalinguistic awareness. Therefore, the errors that this student may produce may not be directly relatable to Tagalog but may, in fact, reflect errors that other language learners from a variety of linguistic backgrounds, make.

An application of the idea is that in order to promote interlanguage learning and negotiation, students should engage in *interlanguage talk* (Long & Porter, 1985). When language learners work with each other in small groups, both the quantity and quality of their speech is better than in individual work or teacher-directed activities (Long & Porter, 1985). More opportunities to practice means more opportunities for students to fine-tune their evolving linguistic knowledge.

See also: Fossilization, Universal Grammar (UG).

Long, M. H., & Porter, P. A. (1985). Group work, interlanguage talk, and second language acquisition. *TESOL Quarterly*, 19(2), 207–228.
Selinker, L. (2014). Interlanguage 40 years on: Three themes from here. In Z. Han & E. Tarone (Eds.), *Interlanguage: Forty years later* (pp. 229–263). John Benjamins.
Tarone, E. (2012). Interlanguage. In *The encyclopedia of applied linguistics* (pp. 1–7). Blackwell.

L1 which stands for "first language", is a term used to describe a speakers' natal language while the term L2, which stands for "second language," refers to the language an individual is additionally learning.

There are other terms that are often interchangeably used with L1 such as *primary language, home language, native language, or mother tongue*. Other terms that are often interchangeably used with L2 include *second language, foreign language, additional language, or target language*.

As with most terms, each of these words has a distinct connotation and may not apply to all learners. For example, the term *mother tongue* carries the connotation of language learned from family and can be a cornerstone of one's identity (Yadav, 2014). The term *target language* is the language taught in an instructional setting and is thought of as the instructional target to learn as much of as possible. The terms L1 and L2 were first used to designate individuals who learned the languages sequentially, but these terms do not necessarily apply to individuals growing up with two or more languages simultaneously and therefore other terms are preferred (Baker, 2001).

While teaching students by exposing them to rich and varied input in the target language is the goal, it is also important to understand that good language teaching is not monolingual (using the target or additional language exclusively). Using a student's L1 (mother tongue, primary or home language) or encouraging them to maintain and use their home language, is important for a student's positive sense of identity and growth. For example, proponents of flexible language use argue that the practice of using the home and additional language is not only effective in giving students access to language and content in the classroom (Celic & Seltzer, 2012), it also helps students develop metalinguistic awareness between and across languages.

See also: Bilinguals (types of), Translanguaging.

Baker, C. (2001). *Foundations of bilingual education and bilingualism* (3rd ed.). Multilingual Matters.
Celic, C., & Seltzer, K. (2012). *Translanguaging: A CUNY-NYSIEB guide for educators*. https://www.wortreich-sprachbildung.de/fileadmin/wortreich_media/Download/Handreichung_Translanguaging.pdf
He, A. E. (2012). Systematic use of mother tongue as learning/teaching resources in target language instruction. *Multilingual Education, 2*(1), 1–15.
Yadav, M. K. (2014). Role of mother tongue in second language learning. *International Journal of Research, 1*(11), 572–582.

Language domains refer to the skills of speaking, listening, reading, and writing.

Speaking and writing are often grouped together as "productive skills" (since language is produced when speaking or writing) while listening and reading are known as "receptive skills" (because listening and speaking involve receiving information from an outside source). These domains are often discussed in pedagogy for English learners because it is widely accepted that teachers should aim to instruct a balance of these skills, and further knowing about these skills can help instructors plan for their instruction (Weed & Diaz-Rico, 1995). Especially with young learners, the development of the domains in an additional language closely resembles the process of acquiring the language domains in your first language. Specifically, the ability to listen often develops first, then speaking; reading and writing may take more time or more exposure to the language to develop (Lightbown & Spada, 2013; Freeman & Freeman, 2014). That said, the development of the skills are interdependent. This interdependence is especially evident in second language learning situations or with older students. Oral skills influence writing development (Schleppegrell, 1996) and writing instruction improves reading comprehension. Instruction integrating the multiple domains of language has been shown to facilitate ELLs' overall academic development.

Integrated skills refers to a lesson, course, or textbook that integrates the four skills of reading, writing, listening, and speaking. Such lesson or material is designed so that there is a connection among the four skills and students have the opportunity to practice all of them (Burns & Siegel, 2018). To illustrate, *Interchange* (Richards et al., 2017) is one of the several textbooks that uses integrated skills. For instance, in one chapter, students may listen to a conversation among friends who discuss their exercise routine and healthy habits. As speaking activities, in addition to role playing the conversations, students may take a poll to find out the fitness programs their classmates have. They may also discuss their own routines as well as favorite Olympic sports and famous athletes in their countries. They may write a short paragraph on one of the topics they discussed. For reading, they may read each other's paragraphs and/or a passage on health and fitness which may include questions. Two popular approaches that use integrated-skills are content-based language instruction and task-based instruction (Oxford, 2001). Some advantages of teaching integrated skills include the ability to work on real life topics and content by using authentic language in tasks that promote interactive communication. It also gives teachers the opportunity to assess the students' four skills.

Notably, speaking, listening, reading, and writing are not the only ways we can make meaning. Now more than ever with the increased use of technology in everyday communication (Johnson, 2014), many texts children and adults interact with are multimodal. Multimodality refers to the concept that meaning-making involves the simultaneous use of multiple modes to convey information, express ideas, and interact with others (Kress & Van Leeuwen, 2001). In interpersonal communication, facial expressions, gestures, tone, movement, and other paralinguistic features also play a role in conveying or deciphering a message. It is important for educators to expose students to a variety of multimodal texts to create a rich environment for learning language across and beyond the four traditional domains.

See also: Stages of Second Language Acquisition.

Burns, A., & Siegel, J. (2018). Teaching the four language skills: Themes and issues. In A. Burns & J. Siegel (Eds.), *International perspectives on teaching the four skills in ELT: Listening, speaking, reading, writing* (pp. 1–20). Palgrave Macmillan.

Diaz-Rico, L. T., & Weed, K. Z. (1995). *The crosscultural, language, and academic development handbook*. Allyn and Bacon.

Freeman, D. E., & Freeman, Y. S. (2014). *Essential linguistics: What teachers need to know to teach ESL, reading, spelling, grammar* (2nd ed.). Heinemann.

Johnson, D. (2014). *Reading, writing, and literacy 2.0*. Teachers College Press.

Kress, G. R., & Van Leeuwen, T. (2001). *Multimodal discourse: The modes and media of contemporary communication*. Cambridge University Press.

Lightbown, P., & Spada, N. M. (2013). *How languages are learned* (4th ed.). Oxford University Press.

Oxford, R. (2001). Integrated skills in the ESL/EFL classroom. *ESL Magazine, 4*(1), 18–20.

Richards, J., Hull, J., & Proctor S. (2017). *Interchange* (5th ed.). Cambridge.

Schleppegrell, M. J. (1996). Conjunction in spoken English and ESL writing. *Applied Linguistics, 17*(3), 271–285.

Language functions, the purposes for which people use language, have been influential in language teaching and the design of teaching materials.

Language functions refer to key uses of language to achieve specific communicative purposes, such as to make a request, to apologize, to retell, and so on. Certain phrases and discourse patterns are often associated with these language functions. As these purposes are based on common situations, language functions play a prominent role in approaches to teaching and learning with a focus on meaning-making and communication.

Language functions receive special attention in several approaches to language and language teaching. In Halliday's functional account of language, three metafunctions bring into focus all components of meaning-making simultaneously: *ideational function,* what we are trying to communicate; *interpersonal function,* who we are communicating with; and *textual function,* how are we communicating the message (Halliday, 1993). Proponents of Communicative Language Teaching see language learning as developing the linguistic means to perform different kinds of functions, such as to ask directions, recount an experience, etc. (Richards & Rodgers, 2001). In earlier language teaching approaches such as the Notional Functional method (Richards & Rodgers, 2001), and even present-day English Language Development Standards (Gottlieb & Ernst-Slavit, 2014), language functions have been included to link communicative situations with certain phrases or target language features to be taught. Another way that language functions appear in language-focused or content-area classrooms, is through language objectives (Gottlieb & Ernst-Slavit, 2014). Language objectives convey what is expected for a student to know, learn, and do with language by the end of a period of instruction and often include language functions such as recount, describe, explain, argue, and others as observable demonstrations of language ability.

See also: Communicative Language Teaching, Notional Functional Method, Sheltered Instruction, Systemic Functional Linguistics (SFL).

Gottlieb, M., & Ernst-Slavit, G. (2014). *Academic language in diverse classrooms: Definitions and contexts.* Corwin Press.
Halliday, M. A. K. (1993). Towards a language-based theory of learning. *Linguistics and Education, 5*(20), 93–116.
Richards, J. C., & Rodgers, T. S. (2001). *Approaches and methods in language teaching* (2nd ed.). Cambridge University Press.

Language loss refers to the phenomenon of "losing" or regressing in one's home language in the process of acquiring an additional language.

Language loss can pertain to an individual losing language, for example, due to immersion or assimilation to another culture and language. Language loss can also pertain to an entire group losing a language, possibly over several generations.

Language loss often occurs in schools due to English-only policies or subtractive programs that aim to teach English (or another target language) without the support of the first language. These programs often manifest the broader aim of assimilating diverse communities into the larger society. On a global level, language loss can be caused by a wide range of factors, including globalization, which often leads to increased urbanization, environmental destruction, and immigration (Hinton, 2001).

The most prominent example of language loss is what has occurred among Native American communities in North America due to assimilationist policies such as the Indian Boarding School movement (Haynes, 2010). Scholars estimate that before assimilationist education policies were enacted there were hundreds of indigenous languages spoken; now, only 194 remain. Of these 194 native languages, many are still in danger of extinction because they are only spoken by elder members of a tribal community (Haynes, 2010).

At a societal level, language loss can lead to the extinction of languages, eliminating cultural diversity and knowledge systems (Hinton, 2001). At an individual level, language loss can also be detrimental, as research shows that there are academic as well as cognitive (Bialystock et al., 2012) consequences. Experts emphasize that language loss can happen easily when monolingualism is prized over linguistic diversity.

See also: Assimilation and Acculturation, Bilingualism (models of), Language Revitalization.

Bialystok, E., Craik, F. I., & Luk, G. (2012). Bilingualism: Consequences for mind and brain. *Trends in Cognitive Sciences*, *16*(4), 240–250.

Haynes, J. (2010). *What is language loss?* Center for Applied Linguistics Heritage Brief. https://www.cal.org/heritage/pdfs/what-is-language-loss.pdf

Hinton, L. (2001). Language revitalization: An overview. In K. Hale & L. Hinton (Eds.), *The green book of language revitalization in practice* (pp. 3–18). Brill.

Language planning refers to the action of creating policies surrounding language use.

Language planning can be carried out at the macro level through government organizations and institutions, or at the micro level by individuals and groups (Cooper, 1989). An individual's or organization's attitude, or orientation, to language influences language planning. Language orientations are not necessarily explicit in a policy, and yet influences in the most basic sense how we talk about language and language issues, decisions made about language, and how to analyze these decisions (Ricento & Hornberger, 1996). There are three basic orientations to language: (1) *language as problem* (i.e., seeing local languages and language use as standing in the way of minoritized cultural and linguistic groups assimilating into the broader society); (2) *language as right* (i.e., seeing local languages and language use as a basic human and civil right worthy of affirmation or protection); (3) *language as resource* (i.e., seeing local languages as resources not only for their own speakers but for the development and expansion of linguistic resources available in a society more broadly (Ruiz, 1984). Bilingual education and heritage language programs are examples of language planning that treat language as resources.

Policies might exist at the federal and state levels to support bilingual education, and yet, intermediary agents including district administrators and the school community have important roles to play. Teachers themselves are important negotiators of language policy (Menken, & García, 2010). They can wield their influence by monitoring procedures and curricula within the classroom, school, or district, getting community support, and lobbying for state and federal policies that benefit students learning English as an additional language.

See also: Bilingual Education Act (BEA), Castañeda v. Pickard (1978), Common European Framework of Reference (CEFR) for Language, Language Policy, Lau v. Nichols (1974), Native American Languages Act, Plyler v. Doe (1982), Program Models, Seal of Biliteracy.

Cooper, R. L. (1989). *Language planning and social change*. Cambridge University Press.
Menken, K., & García, O. (Eds.). (2010). *Negotiating language education policies: Educators as policymakers*. Routledge.
Ricento, T. K., & Hornberger, N. H. (1996). Unpeeling the onion: Language planning and policy and the ELT professional. *TESOL Quarterly*, 30(3), 401–427.
Ruiz, R. (1984). Orientations in language planning. *NABE Journal*, 8(2), 15–34.

Language policy refers to decisions about language, language use, and the teaching and learning of languages.

Language policy can be formal and official or informal with the intent of influencing stakeholders like educators and administrators, community members, or the wider public (Cooper, 1989). Language policy spans three dimensions: (1) changing the form of a language, including the standardization of language, developing a writing system for a spoken language, or coining new words and terms (known as *corpus planning*); (2) modifying the status and prestige of a language, for example, by designation as an official language (known as *status planning*); and (3) developing new users of the language (known as *acquisition planning*). Acquisition planning is relevant to those interested in language learning because it pertains to the teaching and learning of language in school-based settings and beyond.

The field of language policy grew out of the language needs and issues in newly independent, former colonial nations as they planned for how languages would be used and taught, including the colonial or local indigenous languages (Fishman et al., 1968). Most countries have an official language(s), while fewer countries, including the United States, do not have an official language and dominant language is the *de facto* national language.

Some of the most fundamental concerns for language educators–such as what to teach, how to teach, and why—are all policy issues (Ricento & Hornberger, 1996). Teachers make decisions on a daily basis inside the classroom that that both shape and are shaped by society outside of the classroom (Ricento & Hornberger, 1996). The availability of home language instruction, teacher training, support services, and other resources for students learning English as an additional language at school are determined by policies that are made by decisions at the federal, state, or local levels.

See also: Bilingual Education Act (BEA), Castañeda v. Pickard (1978), Common European Framework of Reference (CEFR) for Language, Language Planning, Lau v. Nichols (1974), Native American Languages Act, Plyler v. Doe (1982).

Cooper, R. L. (1989). *Language planning and social change.* Cambridge University Press.
Fishman, J. A., Ferguson, C. A., & Das Gupta, J. (Eds.). (1968). *Language problems of developing nations.* Wiley.
Ricento, T. K., & Hornberger, N. H. (1996). Unpeeling the onion: Language planning and policy and the ELT professional. *TESOL Quarterly, 30*(3), 401–427.

Language revitalization refers to the efforts to save an endangered language from extinction.

Increased monolingualism due to globalization and legacy of European colonization that often continues to disenfranchise indigenous peoples, cultures and language; and various environmental factors (urbanization and natural disasters) are thought to be root causes of language loss. Moreover, half of the world's population now speaks one of thirteen languages (Pine & Turin, 2017); and immigration often causes people to give up their language in the efforts to assimilate to another culture (Hinton, 2001).

Language revitalization efforts aim to reverse this trend. A striking example of language revitalization comes from the restoration of spoken Hebrew which was brought back into use with the founding of the Israeli state after World War II (Hinton, 2001; Turin & Pine). Language revitalization is being accomplished by using various methods, such as enlisting the help of elders to teach/mentor younger members of the community in the language and designing teaching materials for language immersion programs for teaching and learning the endangered language (Pine & Turin, 2017); and designing and implementing bilingual programs for young learners of the language.

Hinton (2001) recommends that any language community take steps to save a language including surveying the community and analyzing how much, if at all, the language is in use; recording the speech of speakers of the language (often elders); creating pedagogical materials to teach the language; create and implement learning programs for learners using the, encouraging use of the language at home, and, lastly, broadening the use of the language in the community (government, media and commercial spaces). While there are many pedagogical approaches to encourage language revitalization, from bilingual programs to language and culture programs for adults, the key is a committed, realistic and methodical approach to the effort (Hinton, 2001).

See also: Language Loss, Language Planning, Language Policy, Native American Languages Act.

Hinton, L. (2001). Language revitalization: An overview. In K. Hale & L. Hinton (Eds.), *The green book of language revitalization in practice* (pp. 3–18). Brill.

Pine, A., & Turin, M. (2017). *Language revitalization. Oxford research encyclopedia of linguistics.* Oxford University Press.

Language transfer is the influence that one language can have in the learning process of another.

Language transfer used to be seen as the source of errors in second language acquisition. Today, however, language transfer is seen more as a natural part of the process of acquiring a second language. It is very natural for learners to try to access the language knowledge they have, i.e., knowledge of language conventions of their L1, to try to convey meaning in their L2 (Lee & Van Patten, 2000). In terms of the production results, language transfer can be positive or negative. In other words, while the similarities that the languages have can facilitate the language acquisition, their differences may interfere negatively and lead to errors (Richards & Schmidt, 2010). However, errors are mostly seen as a natural and necessary part of the process (Lee & Van Patten, 2000). These similarities and dissimilarities can be in several aspects of language learning such as grammar structure, pronunciation, and vocabulary (Freeman & Freeman, 2014). For example, Arabic speakers when learning English may use the word *before* when they mean *ago* and say, "I ate pizza for dinner before three days." They will say so because that is how this sentence is structured in Arabic. They might also pronounce the "p" in pizza as a /b/ sound since the /p/ is inexistent in Arabic. An example of positive language interference can be seen in the use of *if-clauses* since languages like Portuguese and Spanish construct those clauses exactly the same way it is done in English. Therefore, when learning *if*-clauses, those learners will reach out to the knowledge they have in their L1, and that will facilitate the acquisition of if-cluses in English. It is important that teachers are aware of not only the existence of language interference but also of the likely errors that students from a given language background will make. This knowledge empowers teachers to use language interference as a beneficial tool in the teaching-learning process.

See also: Common Underlying Proficiency (CUP), Interlanguage, Metalinguistic Awareness.

Freeman, E. D., & Freeman, Y. S. (2014). *Essential linguistics: what teachers need to know to teach ESL, reading, spelling, grammar* (2nd ed.). Heinemann.

Lee, F. J., & Van Patten, B. (2003). *Making communicative language teaching happen* (2nd ed.). McGraw-Hill.

Richards, J. C., & Schmidt, R. (2010). *The Longman dictionary of language teaching & applied linguistics* (4th ed.). Pearson.

Lau v. Nichols (1974) was the U.S. Supreme Court Case which stated that non-English speaking students were being denied a meaningful education, due to the curriculum being designed for fluent English speakers with no accommodations for English learners.

This U.S. Supreme Court case was brought to court by 18,000 non-English speaking students in San Francisco. They argued that they were being denied an equal education since the curriculum was in a language they did not understand. The case was decided based on Title VI of the Civil Right Act of 1964 since the plaintiffs were from a national-origin minority group.

Under the school curriculum in place at the time of Lau v. Nichols (1974), harm was claimed under three broad areas: psychological harm, educational harm, and economic and political harm. Psychological harm was caused by the isolation and stigmatization of students' inability to participate in classroom activities. Educational harm was a result of not being able to access the curriculum and therefore being put in remedial classes and having to repeat grade levels unnecessarily. Economic and political harm came into play since these students without high school diplomas were forced to take low paying jobs and their lack of English proficiency inhibited their participation in the political process (Sugarman & Widess, 1974).

While the case was heard over 50 years ago, it still has ramifications for today. Even in the 21st Century, the Department of Health, and Human Services (2000) issued guidelines requiring districts to take affirmative action to ensure access to quality education for non-proficient English-speaking students. Guidelines required public schools to provide English as a second language or bilingual programs to help these students learn English and gain access to content of instruction.

See also: Casañeda v. Pickard (1981), Language Policy, Language Planning, Pyler v. Doe (1982).

Health and Human Services Department. (2000, August 30). Title VI of the Civil Rights Act of 1964; Policy guidance on the prohibition against national origin discrimination as it affects persons with Limited English Proficiency. *Federal Register, 65*(169).

Sugarman, S. D., & Widess, E. G. (1974). Equal protection for non-English-speaking school children: Lau v. Nichols. *California Law Review, 62*(1), 157–182.

Wright, W. E. (2019). *Foundations for teaching English language learners: Research, theory, policy and practice* (3rd ed.). Caslon.

Linguistics is an academic discipline referring to the systematic inquiry of human language.

The branches of linguistics include: (1) phonology—the study of a language's sound system; (2) morphology—the study of words and word parts; (3) syntax—the study of how words and phrases are arranged to create sentences; (4) semantics—the study of meaning; (5) pragmatics—the study of language use.

Scholars argue that it is important for teachers of English learners to understand linguistics or to possess *pedagogical language knowledge* (Galguera, 2011) to effectively teach the language and literacy required to teach content specific knowledge. Other scholars argue that by understanding linguistics, specifically the structure of English and other languages, as well as the developmental progression of second language acquisition, teachers are better equipped to plan lessons, evaluate students, give them corrective feedback, and to have an appreciation of other languages and cultures to help students learn in culturally sustaining and affirming ways (Wong Fillmore & Snow, 2002). Linguistic knowledge of different discourse styles can also assist a teacher in effective teaching and promoting student engagement in linguistically and culturally diverse classrooms. By honoring students' use of social varieties outside the classroom, teachers can build a bridge to the academic variety primarily used in the school setting. Linguistic research shows that students can develop multiple dialects and use the appropriate one in the corresponding setting (Burridge & Stebbins, 2020).

See also: Morphology, Phonology, Pragmatics, Semantics, Syntax.

Burridge, K., & Stebbins, T. N. (2020). *For the love of language: An introduction to linguistics* (2nd ed.). Cambridge University Press.
Fillmore, L. W., & Snow, C. (2002). What teachers need to know about language. In C. T. Adger, C. E. Snow, & D. Christian (Eds.), *What teachers need to know about language* (pp. 7–53). Multilingual Matters.
Galguera, T. (2011). Participant structures as professional learning tasks and the development of pedagogical language knowledge among preservice teachers. *Teacher Education Quarterly*, *38*(1), 85–106.

Long-Term English Learner (L-TEL) refers to an English learner who has received most or all of their formal K-12 educational instruction (6–7 years or more) in English who requires ongoing support in English, often academic language, in order to meet academic requirements.

The term L-TEL first appears in the literature in the early 2010s and by 2014, Olsen (2014) argues that this group of English learners has been particularly "unnoticed and their needs unaddressed in a time of strong accountability measures, intense scrutiny of student achievement, and major school improvement initiatives" (p. 3). Notably, these students are often middle and high school students who are fluent in other social registers of language. At the same time, they should have access to grade level content courses so that they do not fall behind in critical subject areas. Absent these interventions, L-TELs are often placed in low academic tracks where they are more likely to fail or drop out of school (Callahan, 2005).

While proponents of this term may point out that L-TEL draws attention to the diversity and diverse needs of language learners, critics argue that this term may have a negative impact on this subgroup of English learners by underestimating their academic and linguistic abilities by keeping them in remedial tracks for too long (Thompson, 2015). These critics also are suspect of the validity of testing to measure language proficiency, arguing that the unique linguistic strengths of L-TELs are, in fact, far more fluid, dynamic and stronger, than assessments can capture.

See also: English Learner (EL), Students with Limited or Interrupted Education (SLIFE).

Callahan, R. M. (2005). Tracking and high school English learners: Limiting opportunity to learn. *American Educational Research Journal, 42*(2), 305–328.
Olsen, L. (2010). *Reparable harm: Fulfilling the unkept promise of educational opportunity for long-term English learners*. Californians Together.
Olsen, L. (2014). Meeting the unique needs of long-term English language learners. *National Education Association, 1*(1), 1–36.
Thompson, K. (2015). Questioning the long-term English learner label: How categorization can blind us to students' abilities. *Teachers College Record, 117*(12), 1–50.
Valdés, G., Poza, L., & Brooks, M. D. (2014). *Educating students who do not speak the societal language: The social construction of language learner categories*. MLA Profession. https://profession.mla.org/educating-students-who-do-not-speak-the-societal-language-the-social-construction-of-language-learner-categories/

Metalinguistic awareness is conscious thinking about how language works.

There are many elements of language that a language user or learner may be aware of. Semantic awareness entails awareness of meaning, phonological awareness involves awareness of the sound system, syntactic awareness pertains to awareness of word order, and pragmatic awareness refers to awareness of how language is used in and influenced by context (Bialystok, 2001; Tunmer et al., 1984). As children grow and their language matures, they are more able to consciously notice and talk about language. The ability to reflect on language enhances the ability to learn a new language. Bilinguals tend to be especially aware of their language use. Early studies with bilingual children showing high levels of word awareness, semantic development, and sentence construction compared with monolingual peers (García, 2009).

Teachers can promote the development of metalinguistic awareness through several means. They can show their own thinking process through "think alouds" while reflecting on some aspect of language and encourage students to explain their own thought process when deciding what words or conventions to use. Showing students several examples of language that follow a certain phonetic or grammatical pattern can also help students notice and articulate a certain aspect of how language works. Having students compare meanings, sounds, or word order in two languages is an especially effective means of developing metalinguistic awareness because it affirms students' knowledge of one language while learning more about the additional language. To carry out these strategies, it can help for teachers to have familiarity with more than one language or at the very least encourage students to make those connections with questions that promote reflection (e.g., how would you say that in your language, do any of these words, phrases, or endings that look like/sound like this in a language you know?).

See also: Cognates, Noticing Hypothesis, Translanguaging.

Bialystok, E. (2001). *Bilingualism in development: Language, literacy, and cognition*. Cambridge University Press.
García, O. (2009). *Bilingual education in the 21st century: A global perspective*. John Wiley & Sons.
Tunmer, W., Pratt, C., & Herriman, M. (1984). *Metalinguistic awareness in children*. Springer.

Migrant education refers to specialized educational programs and initiatives that promote the social, academic, and professional advancement of migratory children and adults.

A migrant is broadly defined by the United Nations as an individual residing away from one's "usual place of residence," regardless of "legal status," the "length of stay," or whether the move is "voluntary or involuntary" (UNESCO, 2021). Migrant education is often aimed at short-term or seasonal migrants, individuals who move to another country or region temporarily or who move back and forth between locations. The educational needs of these migratory children and adults are unique.

Continuous mobility and adaption present many difficulties, especially for adults without formal education and literacy skills. Studies show that migratory adults engaged in jobs requiring lower literacy requirements, such as agriculture or janitorial work, often work in isolation, limiting opportunities for career advancement or interaction with speakers of the host language (Haznedar et al., 2018). Many of these adults have family and work commitments that prevent them from devoting as much time as school-aged children to developing more advanced language and literacy skills.

Children who are themselves migratory workers or who are the children of such workers, similarly face numerous educational challenges. They may start the school day late, leave early, or miss long periods of school during the academic year (Office of English Language Acquisition, 2021). They may also encounter linguistic and cultural barriers, economic instability, and access to continuous health care.

Migrant education programs play a crucial role in providing specialized assistance to address these challenges. These programs encompass a range of services, including remedial and compensatory education; language and literacy courses; vocational training and career education services; counseling and testing services; health services; childcare or preschool services, and academic instruction. The scope and duration of these programs vary widely depending on the national and local context (Bartlett, 2015).

In the United States, the Migrant Education Program is authorized by Title I of the Elementary and Secondary Education Act (ESEA), the country's national education law. Since frequent moves between schools or states is not uncommon among migratory children, the aim of the Migrant Education Program offerings is to help ensure that these children are not penalized by disparities among states in curriculum, graduation requirements, or academic and achievement standards and assessments (Migrant Education Program, n.d.).

Migratory children are five times more likely to qualify for English language development services at school (Office of English Language Acquisition, 2021). To work with migratory students, specialized knowledge of second language development and pedagogy are needed as well as coordination with a broad base of programs and services. Given the international nature of migrant education, the United Nations has identified a number of priorities to effectively serve migratory students. Strategies include a strong emphasis on robust early education efforts, sustained attention to language development, the implementation of culturally responsive pedagogies that build on students' existing knowledge, and a focus on academic and vocational programs that prepare students for further education or the labor market (Bartlett, 2015). These strategies underscore the global importance of addressing the educational needs of migratory populations and the multifaceted approach necessary to ensure their success.

See also: Newcomer Program, Students with Limited Formal Education (SLIFE)

Bartlett, L. (2015). *Access and quality of education for international migrant children.* Paper commissioned for the EFA Global Monitoring Report, 2000–2015.

Haznedar, B., Peyton, J. K., & Young-Scholten, M. (2018). Teaching adult migrants: A focus on the languages they speak. *Critical Multilingualism Studies, 6*(1), 155–183.

Migrant Education Program (n.d.). https://results.ed.gov/about

Office of English Language Acquisition. (2021). *Migratory children who are English learners.* https://ncela.ed.gov/resources/fact-sheet-migratory-children-who-are-english-learners-june-2021

UNESCO. (2021, September 23). *Migrants, refugees, or displaced person?* https://www.unesco.org/en/articles/migrants-refugees-or-displaced-persons

Monitor hypothesis is a theory that posits that language learners have an internal monitor that regulates their language use for correctness.

The monitor hypothesis is one of Krashen's (1982) well-known hypotheses about how language learners acquire an additional language. In this hypothesis there is a shift from pure acquisition of language, the basis of his model, to more conscious language learning. When using a language, we monitor and subsequently edit our language for what "sounds right" based on our acquisition and using rules we have learned (Freeman & Freeman, 2014).

Krashen (1982) states that for the language learner's monitor to be effective, the individual must have (1) time to process and formulate what to say, (2) the form and appropriateness of what they want to express, and (3) the grammatical rules to determine if how they are speaking is correct. He also maintains that there are monitor "over-users" who are too focused on correctness to be able to communicate sufficiently to be comprehensible (i.e., speak with halted fluency), and monitor "under-users" who may speak with too little regard for form or correctness. The effective monitor, by this argument, provides a "just right" amount of internal editing, but not too much as to prevent the speaker from using and acquiring language.

Critics of the monitor hypothesis argue that the theory lacks coherence (Gregg, 1984). It is also difficult to prove in spoken language, as, in a single utterance, it is impossible to distinguish between what has been produced because of acquisition, and what is the result of monitored language (Lightbown & Spada, 2021). Writing, on the other hand, may be more conductive for learners to monitor language and for teachers to detect the monitor at work. Ultimately, the monitor hypothesis can help sensitize teachers to the complex process of producing accurate spoken language and guide learners to focus on expression in balance with striving for correctness.

See also: Error Correction, Noticing Hypothesis.

Freeman, D. E., & Freeman, Y. S. (2014). *Essential linguistics: What teachers need to know to teach ESL, reading, spelling, grammar* (2nd ed.). Heinemann.
Gregg, K. R. (1984). Krashen's monitor and Occam's razor. *Applied linguistics*, 5(2), 79–100.
Krashen, S. (1982). *Principles and practice in second language acquisition*. Oxford University Press.
Lightbown, P. M., & Spada, N. (2021). *How languages are learned* (5th ed.). Oxford University Press.

Morphology refers to the study of words and word parts.

Morpheme is a term from morphology meaning the smallest meaningful unit. Morphemes can be stand-alone words or word parts that change the word's meaning. Free morphemes carry meaning of their own, for example, a word like *tree* or *apple*. These are often the roots of words. Bound morphemes, in contrast, do not carry meaning unless they are attached to a free morpheme. These include affixes, that is, prefixes and suffixes. Suffixes can be further categorized into *inflectional suffixes* that change the form of the word like the -s or -es of a plural or the -ed to form the past tense of a word. Derivational affixes change the meaning of a word and include prefixes (*inter-* in international) or suffixes (*-ment* in commencement).

One benefit of understanding morphology is to gain insight into word history (the etymology of words) as well as similarities and differences between languages. Linguists classify languages based on how words are formed. In English, for example, numerous words have endured from Old English (like father and sparrow) or are borrowed from other languages, predominantly French and Latin (Freeman & Freeman, 2014).

Teachers can incorporate morphological perspectives in vocabulary instruction by teaching students to observe and learn word parts (prefixes, root words, and suffixes). Understanding morphology can also help students better understand novel vocabulary in sentences or manipulate the part of speech of a word, a process known as nominalization, changing a word from a verb or an adjective to a noun (for example, to change a verb like "refuse" to the noun "refusal"). Lastly, scholars recommend that teachers teach cognates, or shared words between languages (Williams, 2001). These strategies, along with explicit vocabulary instruction, can help students to meet the demands of reading, writing, and speaking in academic environments.

See also: Linguistics, Vocabulary Teaching and Learning.

Freeman, D. E., & Freeman, Y. S. (2014). *Essential linguistics: What teachers need to know to teach ESL, reading, spelling, grammar* (2nd ed.). Heinemann.

Williams, J. (2001). Classroom conversations: Opportunities to learn for ESL students in mainstream classrooms. *The Reading Teacher, 54*(8), 759–757.

Native American Languages Act (1990) reserves the right of indigenous groups to use, practice, and develop their native language and culture within the U.S. education system.

The Native American Languages Act (NALA) is U.S. federal policy allowing the use of Native American languages as the medium of instruction in schools and affirms the rights of indigenous students to express themselves, be educated, and be assessed using their native languages. The rationale was to address Native American educational rights as well as the increase in the Native American educator community (McCarty, 2013).

This legislation attempts to repair the damage done by the Dawes Act of 1887 which allowed the federal government to break up tribal lands. From the 1870s to the 1970s, Native Americans experienced a significant loss in control of their education, as they were forced to enroll in boarding schools designed for assimilation (McCarty, 2013). Children were punished, physically and psychologically, for using their own language instead of using English.

Prior to NALA, Native American language protections were established through the Elementary and Secondary Education Act (ESEA) of 1966 and the Bilingual Education Act (BEA) of 1968. In 1990, NALA was passed, followed by a grant program in 1992 to support Native Americans and Native Hawai'ians to preserve their languages. The Esther Martinez Native American Languages Preservation Act of 2006 further enhanced funding for initiatives like language nests, master-apprentice programs, immersion camps, curriculum development, teacher training, and parental language classes.

The 2001 reauthorization of ESEA, known as the No Child Left Behind Act, raises concerns due to its English-focused teaching and testing (Klug, 2012). However, it is important to note that NALA holds special significance because it formally recognizes the cultural wealth of Native Americans and that native languages are as important as instruction in any other language.

See also: Bilingual Education Act (BEA), Language Planning, Language Policy, Language Loss, Language Revitalization.

Klug, B. J. (2012). *Standing together: American Indian education as culturally responsive pedagogy.* R&L Education.
McCarty, T. L. (2013). *Language planning and policy in Native America: History, theory, praxis* (Vol. 90). Multilingual Matters.

Native Speaker (NS) and Nonnative Speaker (NNS) are terms often used to make the distinction between those who have learned a language as their mother tongue ("native speakers") and those who have learned English as an additional language ("nonnative speakers").

Distinguishing between NS and NNS is a thorny issue in TESOL. Given the widespread influence of English due to colonization and globalization, determining 'nativeness' or 'nonnativeness' based on birthplace and first language is considered insufficient (Liu, 1999). Some argue that the native/nonnative distinction is a fallacy, acknowledging the vast variation in language ability, even among native monolinguals (Canagarajah, 1999). Nevertheless, this distinction perpetuates the notion that NS are more proficient and entitled to greater language ownership. Alternative definitions extend beyond birthplace and language acquisition order. Identity, status, and confidence in relation to a language also contribute to characterizing groups of speakers (Davies, 1991).

For teachers of the English language, the dichotomy also poses challenges. Labels like "native English-speaking teacher" (NEST) and "nonnative English-speaking teacher" (NNEST) carry racial, hegemonic, and imperialist undertones (Holliday & Aboshiha, 2009). While learners of a language often excel at teaching the language, the term "non-native" can induce feelings of inadequacy among these teachers. Furthermore, professional opportunities for NNEST can be jeopardized by the perceived contrast with NEST as the "ideal" language teacher (Mackenzie, 2020). An alternative phrase, "English teachers who learned English as an additional language," has been proposed (Blum & Johnson, 2012).

See also: English as a lingua franca, L1 and L2, World Englishes

Blum, A., & Johnson, E. J. (2012). Reading repression: Textualizing the linguistic marginalization of nonnative English-speaking teachers in Arizona. *Journal of Language, Identity, and Education, 11*, 167–184.

Canagarajah, A. S. (1999). Interrogating the "native speaker fallacy": Non-linguistic roots, non-pedagogical results. In G. Braine (Ed.), *Nonnative educators in English language teaching* (pp.77–92). Lawrence Erlbaum.

Davies, A. (1991). *The native speaker in applied linguistics*. Edinburgh University Press.

Holliday, A., & Aboshiha, P. (2009). The denial of ideology in perceptions of 'nonnative speaker' teachers. *TESOL Quarterly, 43*(4), 669–689.

Liu, J. (1999). Nonnative-English-speaking professionals in TESOL. *TESOL Quarterly, 33*(1), 85–102.

Mackenzie, L. (2020). Discriminatory job advertisements for English language teachers in Colombia: An analysis of recruitment biases. *TESOL Journal, 12*(1).

Natural Approach (NA) utilizes exposure to comprehensible input ($i+1$) in order for students to acquire a second language by communicating naturally.

The Natural Approach is one example of a communicative approach to second language acquisition because it emphasizes vocabulary and meaning rather than explicit teaching of grammatical structures as with, for example, the Grammar Translation Method.

NA is a result of the combination of Tracy Terrell's teaching experience and Stephen Krashen's theory of second language acquisition, which culminated in the publishing of the book *The Natural Approach* in 1983.

To provide comprehensible input and express meanings in the target language, teachers may use a variety of techniques such as realia, images, objects and other manipulatives, and body language. The input level of complexity increases as students move up levels. To illustrate, students can be asked yes/no questions at lower levels and information questions subsequently (Freeman & Freeman 2014).

The innovation that the Natural Approach has brought to the field is not present in its techniques, but in the emphasis it places on comprehension and meaningfulness rather than of perfectly structured sentences with flawless grammar (Richards & Rodgers, 2001). According to the Natural Approach, effective second and foreign language classrooms foster an environment where learners are not only provided with appropriate comprehensible input, but also where they can communicate meaningfully, intelligibly, and as its name states, naturally (Richards & Rodgers, 2001).

See also: Communicative Language Teaching (CLT), Input Hypothesis

Freeman, D. E., & Freeman Y. S. (2014). *Essential linguistics: What teachers need to know to teach ESL, reading, spelling, grammar* (2nd ed.). Heinemann.
Richards, J. C., & Rodgers, T. S. (2001). *Approaches and methods in language teaching* (2nd ed.). Cambridge University Press.

Natural order hypothesis states that both the first and second languages are acquired in a certain order.

Krashen (1982) proposed that additional languages are acquired much in the same way as one's first language, that is, without conscious attention to learning. A second part of this theory is that a similarly predictable sequence is followed for those acquiring additional languages, regardless of the language background of the learner. For example, present and past progressive verb tenses (is swimming, was swimming) are acquired before irregular past tense conjugations (swam) and adding an -s to mark a plural object (books) is acquired before the possessive case (Min's book). However, when two languages have very similar structures, the acquisition of morphemes might break with the expected order (Lightbown & Spada, 2013). For example, the possessive case in German and English is similar (*das kinds bett*=the child's bed), so adding -s for the possessive case might be acquired more readily than adding -s for plurals. Researchers have conducted cross-linguistic analyses to identify specific developmental stages and the variations among languages (e.g., Wode, 1978).

Critics of this hypothesis argue that languages aren't easily "picked up" with the subconscious seamlessness that Krashen suggests. Instead, they argue that languages are skills that need to be taught explicitly and practiced for the brain use with automaticity (Lightbown & Spada, 2013). However, the general idea that some language patterns are more easily acquired than others, can inform teachers' decisions about what to teach and when.

See also: Monitor Hypothesis, Natural Approach, Second Language Acquisition Theory, Stages of Second Language Acquisition.

Krashen, S. (1982). *Principles and practice in second language acquisition*. Oxford University Press.

Lightbown, P., & Spada, N. M. (2013). *How languages are learned* (4th ed.). Oxford University Press.

Wode, H. (1981). Language acquisitional universals: A unified view of language acquisition. In H. Winitz (Ed.), *Native language and foreign language acquisition* (pp. 218–234). Annals of the New York Academy of Sciences.

Newcomer program is a term used to refer to programs (predominantly in U.S. K-12 settings) that serve students new to the English language who are refugees and immigrants and new the country.

Newcomer programs are specifically created programs within schools to help newly arrived refugees and immigrants acclimate to the school, culture, and academic concepts. Newcomer programs are aimed to last between approximately 6 months and 2 years (Short & Boyson, 2004). Newcomer programs can consist of separate classes that students take for a part of the school day aimed at helping them make the transition to U.S. culture and schools and to learn the language required for content-area learning. These programs may even operate on separate sites or be stand-alone schools (Hoh, 2020; Short & Boyson, 2004).

Proponents of newcomer programs argue that, when thoughtfully planned, these programs give students a safe, supportive environment to learn language, as well as the cultural and academic demands of life in their new schools. Further, they learn with peers who are at similar stages of language learning and by learning within a supportive academic environment tailored to their specific experiences and needs (Feinber, 2000; Short & Boyson, 2004). Critics contend that these programs segregate newcomer students from grade-level content (Feinberg, 2004) and as a result these students are often unable to earn the necessary academic credits to advance in school, as newcomer classes frequently do not count toward graduation (Hos, 2020).

See also: Long-Term English Learners (L-TEL), Program Models, Students with Limited or Interrupted Education (SLIFE).

Feinberg, R. C. (2000). Newcomer schools: Salvation or segregated oblivion for immigrant students? *Theory Into Practice, 39*, 220–227.
Hos, R. (2020). The lives, aspirations, and needs of refugee and immigrant Students with Interrupted Formal Education (SIFE) in a secondary newcomer program. *Urban Education, 55*(7), 1021–1044.
Short, D., & Boyson, B. A. (2004). *Creating access: Language and academic programs for secondary school newcomers.* Center for Applied Linguistics.

Noticing Hypothesis refers to the idea that the first step in learning something new in a language (vocabulary word, sentence structure, verb conjugation, etc.) is noticing it for oneself.

The Noticing Hypothesis suggests that, independent of instruction, the learner noticing a linguistic phenomenon is essential for acquiring it. Furthermore, researchers have looked at the components of noticing, such as alertness, understanding/registering when new information is coming in, developmental readiness, and how attention is directed (Robinson, 1995).

While this idea seems to provide a necessary insight that acquiring a new language has to be driven by the learner's perceptions and readiness to learn, this idea is hard to substantiate with formal research studies. However, researchers have designed studies that have learners reflecting on their own videotaped conversations (Mackey, Gass, & McDonough, 2000). In that way, learners are able to provide insights into their own language use, offering researchers valuable perspectives on how learners engage in the process of noticing linguistic elements.

Despite different views in second language research as to the necessity of conscious attention, there are practical implications for the noticing hypothesis. As an alternative to teacher-centered lecture or "telling," teachers can help students "notice" linguistic features by providing illustrative examples and asking questions to prompt them to recognize the pattern for themselves. The idea is that articulating the pattern or exceptions to the pattern help learners become aware of and internalize the linguistic features. In turn, students are more active in the learning process. "Noticing" as a pedagogical practice can be incorporated into instructional styles to elevate student engagement and vary from teacher-fronted modes of instruction.

See also: Metalinguistic Awareness.

Leow, R. P. (2013). Schmidt's noticing hypothesis: More than two decades after. In J. M. Bergsleithner, S. N. Frota, & J. K. Yoshioka (Eds.), *Noticing and second language acquisition: Studies in honor of Richard Schmidt* (pp. 23–35). National Foreign Language Resource Center.

Mackey, A., Gass, S., & McDonough, K. (2000). How do learners perceive interactional feedback? *Studies in Second Language Acquisition*, 22(4), 471–497.

Robinson, P. (1995). Attention, memory, and the "noticing" hypothesis. *Language Learning*, 45(2), 283–331.

Notional Functional Method is a thematic and incremental way of structuring the teaching of language around "notions," that is, real-life situations in which the target language is likely to be used, and delineated into "functions," or specific aims for communication, and related phrases.

The Notional Functional Method has its beginnings in 1977 when the committee of Out-of School Education as part of the Council of Europe began investigating whether there was an optimal way for adults to learn a language (Ahmed & Alamin, 2012). Language experts subsequently developed the concept of the Threshold Level, the minimal language requirements an adult would need to know and be able to express using the target language in certain real-life situations. This Threshold Level was determined to be approximately a thousand words for productive and receptive language and another five hundred words for recognition only (Van Ek, 1976).

This method is focused on language for situation-specific communication and required extensive analysis to determine the necessary language for a variety of situations such as seeking information, expressing an opinion or attitude, giving advice, or negotiating. Social roles with whom the language would be used were first examined (stranger to stranger, friend to friend, employee to supervisor). These roles were further subdivided into emotions associated with each situation, and identification of the setting and topics which would arise during these interactions. Then the purpose of the communicative interaction was analyzed. Since functions often lend themselves to certain language patterns, semantic and syntactic language needed for each interaction were identified (Ahmed & Alamin, 2012) and associated with a level of difficulty. Since the purpose of the Notional Functional Method was to communicate and function in the target language daily, very little reading and writing of the target language was taught, only basic communicative skills such as reading signs, friendly messages, and filling out forms, etc.

See also: Audio-Lingual Method (ALM), Grammar Translation Method (GRM).

Ahmed, S., & Alamin, A. (2012). The communicative approaches revisited and the relevance of teaching grammar. *English Language Teaching, 5*(1), 2–9.
Van Ek, J. (1976). *The threshold level.* Council of Europe.

Orthography refers to the study of written language, including the development of conventions in spelling, punctuation, spacing, and other features of written language.

Writing systems can be logographic, in which symbols represent meanings as in Egyptian hieroglyphs or like Chinese, which is composed of radicals (symbols that are combined to form a character). Photographic writing systems, on the other hand, are those in which the symbols represent sounds. Among photographic writing systems there's Japanese, with characters that represent syllables (so a syllabic writing system), and English, in which constants and vowels represent syllables (so an alphabetic system). The orthography of English has a complex history so it can be difficult for a learner to know how to correctly spell words based on how they sound, and inversely, it can be difficult to know how to sound out the words while reading (Park-Johnson & Shin, 2020).

There are three reasons a word might have a certain spelling. One reason is phonological, that is, to preserve the sound of the word. For example, the word "sit" is spelled exactly as it sounds and of course there are some exceptions like homophones (great and grate) and while the sound is preserved, the spelling serves to signal the words mean something different. Another reason words are spelled a certain way is semantic, that is, to preserve the meaning of the word. For example, words like breath and breath sound different but are spelled alike to show the words share a similar meaning. Finally, the third reason is etymological, that is, to signal the origin of the word. Some words bear resemblance to their spelling in Old English like father and fæder or there are loanwords (or phrases) from other languages like *déjà vu* which maintains the original spelling from French. Teachers who understand the development and history of English orthography can help learners of the language understand that there are indeed patterns in English spelling and the reasons for these patterns.

See also: Homonyms, Homophones, and Heteronyms.

Freeman, D. E., & Freeman, Y. S. (2014). *Essential linguistics: What teachers need to know to teach ESL, reading, spelling, grammar* (2nd ed.). Heinemann.
Moats, L. C., & Tolman, C. A. (2019). *LETRS* (3rd ed.). Voyager Sopris Learning, Inc.
Park-Johnson, S., & Shin, S. J. (2020). *Linguistics for language teachers: Lessons for classroom practice*. Routledge.

Phonological awareness and phonemic awareness refer to the awareness of sounds in one's language.

More specifically, phonological awareness refers to a person's ability to hear and distinguish words and syllables. There are three levels of phonological awareness: syllable awareness, awareness of onset-rime (the first and ending sounds in a syllable), and awareness of individual sounds, or phonemes. When learners can distinguish which words have the same final sounds or are able to segment sounds into syllables or the reverse, put words together based on separate syllables, they are exhibiting phonological awareness.

While phonological awareness is the broader term, phonemic awareness specifically refers to the knowledge of individual sounds in word, as well as the ability to hear sounds at the beginning, middle or end of words and manipulate them. Students are often taught and assessed in phonemic awareness based on their abilities to add, substitute, or delete sounds from a word. For example, a common substitution task would be something like asking the student to change the first sound of /c/ cat to make mat /m/.

Phonological and phonemic awareness have both been shown to play a critical role in literacy development (Stanovich, 1986). However, while phonological and phonemic awareness are tied to reading skill instruction, linking sounds to the letter system is called phonics instruction. This type of instruction is aimed at helping students decode words instead of guessing. Phonics instruction is often part of an explicit approach to teaching reading in English. It is also important to note that even when a learner has strong phonological awareness or an ability to map this awareness to reading and decode, they may still need exposure to vocabulary and oral language required to make sense of text and participate in discussions (Goldenberg, 2021). It is advisable for teachers to understand phonological and phonemic awareness so that they can evaluate their students' strengths and needs and subsequently identify the most suitable approach for teaching phonology and reading in their classrooms.

See also: Allophones, Phonology.

Goldenberg, C. (2020). Reading wars, reading science, and English learners. *Reading Research*, 55, S131–S144.
Stanovich, K. (1986). Matthew effects in reading: Some consequences of individual differences in the acquisition of literacy. *Reading Research Quarterly, 21*, 360–407.

Phonology, one of the branches of linguistics, is the systematic study of a language's sound system.

To understand the sounds of any language, linguists who specialize in phonology need to identify each individual sound, called phonemes. Phonemes are units of sound in any given language.

English has approximately 40 different phonemes and each sound combines to form words. All the phonemes in the world's languages are classified into two categories: consonants which somehow constrict or stop the airflow when articulated, and vowels that do not constrict air flow. Phonemes are classified according to the International Phonetic Alphabet (IPA) which is a standardized system of symbols representing the district sounds in human language. Phonemes are analyzed by where they are formed in the mouth and vocal tract, and whether they are vowels or consonants. 44 symbols make up the IPA.

While phonemes are familiar and classifiable across languages, each phoneme is made of an even smaller unit of sound called an allophone. An allophone can be a variation of a certain phoneme in terms of where it is articulated in the mouth (where the tongue is placed, how much breath comes out), depending on the sound that comes directly before it. An example of an allophone is the sound of the letter /t/. To appreciate the subtle differences, say the words top, pot, kitten letter, train, and stop to see how the /t/ sound is different across these words (Freeman & Freeman, 2013).

It is important for educators to know about phonemes and the IPA so that they can appreciate the vast diversity of sounds found in human language. Moreover, understanding variations in phonology can help educators understand differences in pronunciation as they discern the best ways to help their students acquire comprehensible pronunciation and as it relates to skills like phonics–the combination of decoding and phonemic awareness–which many argue are essential to learning to read.

See also: Allophones, Phonological Awareness and Phonemic Awareness.

Freeman, D. E., & Freeman, Y. S. (2014). *Essential linguistics: What teachers need to know to teach ESL, reading, spelling, grammar* (2nd ed.). Heinemann.

Plyler v. Doe (1982) is the U.S. Supreme Court decision that made it unconstitutional to deny students a free public education based on their immigration status.

The case had its beginnings in 1975 Texas state legislation that allowed districts to ban foreign born immigrants from U.S. public schools who did not have legal entry to the U.S. This was followed by a Tyler, Texas school policy that these immigrants must pay tuition to attend public schools. A group of Mexican immigrants without documentation of legal immigration filed a class action lawsuit against the school district. A district court found that the policy violated the constitution. In addition, the court referenced then President Carter's proposed immigration amnesty plan which could provide legal status to students currently living in the district without documentation (*Doe v. Plyler*, 1978). Upon appeal, a federal court concurred with the violation of the constitutional rights and the school district filed for review by the Supreme Court which was granted.

The U.S. Supreme Court relied on the Equal Protection clause of the 14th Amendment to the Constitution which affirms that not only must the federal government govern impartially, but states must do so also. Review of this case found that since Texas provided free public education to citizens and legally admitted immigrants to the United States, it could not deny free public education to those who were not in the state legally without demonstrating that it promoted some significant state interest (Yoshino, 2011). The Supreme Court elaborated on the decision by declaring that the denial of free public education to undocumented students harmed the children's interest and indeed society as a whole. Additionally, holding children accountable for the actions of their parents was also highlighted as being contrary to the concept of justice (*Plyler v. Doe*, 1982).

See also: Castañeda v. Pickard (1978), Language Policy, Language Practice, Lau v. Nichols (1974).

Doe v. Plyler, 458 F. Supp. 569 (E.D. Tex. 1978). https://law.justia.com/cases/federal/district-courts/FSupp/458/569/1875816/
Plyler v. Doe, 457 U.S. 202, 206 n.2. (1982).
Yoshino, K. (2011). The new equal protection. *Harvard Law Review*, 124(3), 747–803.

Pragmatics is the study of language use and meaning making in its contextual use.

Linguists who study pragmatics analyze such issues as the multiple meanings of words (called polysemy) or the discrepancy between the literal and figurative meaning of words. This contrast is particularly evident in idiomatic expressions. Another aspect of the study of pragmatics is the analysis of conversations or speech acts. A pioneer of pragmatics argued that human conversation is governed by four rules called maxims (Grice, 1975).

1. Maxim of quality: the speaker must tell the truth and/or have evidence for their claim.
2. Maxim of quantity: the speaker must include enough but not too much information.
3. Maxim of relation: the speaker's contribution must be relevant.
4. Maxim of manner: the speaker must be clear.

When one of these maxims is violated or flouted, the conversation is less likely to be successful.

When applied to second language acquisition and language teaching, understanding how people organize their speech and phrase things in another language can be very important. For example, when a speaker tries to sound polite while making a request or refusing something, they are using their knowledge of pragmatics. Further, even if a speaker knows the correct vocabulary and grammar, they often require guidance in and practice with pragmatics. For teachers, knowledge of pragmatics can be helpful, as they explicitly teach idioms, multiple meanings of language, and have explicit conversations about cues and clues from the context can also help students become aware of how the setting or audience informs language choices. Lastly, giving learners instruction and practice with topics like making polite requests, refusing offers, giving directions, and other common language activities can help build a speaker's confidence in using the language (Bardovi-Harlig, 1996).

See also: Communicative Competence, Figurative Language, Linguistics.

Bardovi-Harlig, K. (1996). Pragmatics and language teaching: Bringing pragmatics and pedagogy together. In L. F. Bouton (Ed.), *Pragmatics and language learning* (Vol. 7, pp. 21–39). University of Illinois.

Grice, H. P. (1975) Logic and conversation. In P. Cole & J. L. Morgan (Eds.), *Syntax and semantics: Speech acts* (pp. 41–58). Academic Press.

Program models are educational programs used for students primarily learning English as an additional language at school.

In general, programs vary by the language used in instruction, duration, and their academic and language goals. Program models have developed and evolved in response to federal, state, and local policy influences as well as research on program effectiveness (Ovando & Combs, 2011). Program names and program implementation have also evolved over time and vary considerably between states, districts, and schools. Included here are concise descriptions of the most common terms used to define English medium of instruction programs and bilingual programs in the United States.

Submersion entails a "sink or swim" approach. Students learning English as an additional language at school are provided with the same instruction and educational services as monolingual students. That is, teachers neither provide alternative services nor use the students' home languages to support their learning. Submersion was prevalent before the 1970s and is the default mode of instruction in the absence of other programs or services (García & Kleifgen, 2010).

Pull-out/Stand-alone provides support for students in special class sessions outside the regular classroom. These sessions are usually taught by a teacher with ESL training and may include some home language support, although this is not always the case. Pull-out, or stand-alone instruction, could focus on English language development or content-area lessons intended to complement or remediate regular classroom instruction. During pull-out or stand-alone instruction, students often miss regular classroom instruction unless planned during a block of time when all students are engaged in individualized supports or interventions.

Push-in/Integrated provides support to students learning English as an additional language at school within the mainstream classroom. The least inclusive version of this model might involve teachers with ESL training tutoring individual students in one corner of the classroom. In a more inclusive arrangement, the ESL and classroom teachers would collaborate and coordinate instruction, enjoy shared planning time, and team teach. Instruction could involve some or no home language support and target English language development or support content-area lessons.

Sheltered instruction, also known as *structured English immersion* or *content-based ESL*, groups students for instruction based on their level of English. Sheltered classes provide targeted content-area instruction by ESL-trained teachers, but this arrangement separates these students from their English-proficient peers. Sheltered instruction is especially prevalent in middle and secondary schools where the routine practice of having multiple sections for different content area classes already exists. English is primarily used as the language for instruction in these programs. The goal is to facilitate English language development without students falling behind academically.

ESL service provision in the mainstream classroom entails ESL-trained teachers serving students learning English as an additional language in the mainstream classroom with their English proficient peers. In this inclusive arrangement, students access grade-level curriculum with English language support. This approach is not considered a specific English-medium of instruction or bilingual program per se, but with increasingly diverse mainstream classrooms and pre-service teacher education programs offering endorsements in TESOL/ESL, classroom teachers providing differentiated instruction to multiple student groups is becoming more common. English is primarily used as the language of instruction; there is no systematic approach to developing the home language, although the teacher or students might use the home language to negotiate meaning. This approach emphasizes English language proficiency and academic achievement.

Transitional bilingual education (TBE), also known as *early exit bilingual education*, develops students' home languages during kindergarten (or PreK) through about 2nd grade. The aim is for students to acquire English as quickly as possible and transition to English-only classrooms without falling behind academically. Teachers in transitional bilingual programs are trained in bilingual education and students receive initial literacy instruction in the home language, some content-area instruction in the home language, and sheltered instruction of some content-areas in English. Initially, the home language is usually used 90% to 50% of the school day. Each year, the amount of instruction in the home language is decreased by about 10% per year while the amount of instruction in English increases. By the end of 2nd grade (or when the program ends), the home language is used about 10% of the day or less (thus also known as the 90/10 model).

Developmental bilingual education (DBE), also known as *late-exit bilingual education*, supports students' development of English and the home language from kindergarten (or PreK) through approximately fourth grade. Teachers in DBE programs are trained in bilingual education and students receive literacy instruction in their home language and English. Often, a language is assigned to certain days, periods of the day, or content-area subjects to ensure concentrated time for developing each language. Initially, the home language might be used 90% of the school day and gradually decrease to 50%, or the home language and English might be used in equal amounts each year from the beginning (known as the 50/50 model). The aims of DBE are bilingualism, biliteracy, and academic achievement.

Two-way bilingual education (TWBE), or *dual language bilingual education, dual language immersion (DLI), or simply dual language,* is notably different from other program models in that students who are English proficient and speakers of a language other than English are taught literacy and content-area subjects in both languages from kindergarten (or PreK) through 4th or 5th grade. Teachers in TWBE programs are trained in bilingual education. Often one teacher is responsible for teaching literacy and content-area subjects in English and one teacher is responsible for teaching literacy and content-area subjects in the other language. Similarly to DBE, the language other than English might be used 90% to 50% of the school day and gradually decrease each year (the 90/10 model), or English and the other target language might be used in equal amounts each year from the beginning (the 50/50 model). TWBE promotes bilingualism, biliteracy, bicultural or critical consciousness (Palmer et al., 2019) and high academic achievement for both groups of students.

See also: Content Language Integrated Learning (CLIL), Newcomer Program, Sheltered Instruction

García, O., & Kleifgen, J. A. (2010). *Educating emergent bilinguals: Policies, programs, and practices for English language learners.* Teachers College Press.

Ovando, C. J., & Combs, M. C. (2011). *Bilingual and ESL classrooms: Teaching in multicultural contexts* (5th ed.). McGraw-Hill.

Palmer, D. K., Cervantes-Soon, C., Dorner, L., & Heiman, D. (2019). Bilingualism, biliteracy, biculturalism, and critical consciousness for all: Proposing a fourth fundamental goal for two-way dual language education. *Theory Into Practice, 58*(2), 121–133.

Scaffolding involves teachers preparing and providing supports that enable students learning English as an additional language at school to understand and express conceptual knowledge of content while their English language proficiency is progressing.

Common ways teachers may scaffold learning for English Learners (ELS) include additional wait time, having students provide responses through graphics or pictorial representations, using their home languages for brainstorms around a topic, working with a partner, and providing sentence frames. Instructional scaffolds, just like construction scaffolds are meant to be temporary and to be removed when no longer needed.

Scaffolds can be grouped into three categories—supporting materials, supportive grouping, and instructional supports (Fenner, 2017). Supportive materials may include English to native language dictionaries, computer read text, sentence frames, and photos/graphics to show meaning of words or processes. Grouping strategies to support ELs may involve partnering an EL student with another student whose English proficiency is more advanced or placing the EL in a small group where s/he has a comfort level with the other group members or asking the EL to explain a word to another student with less English than s/he has. Instructional supports may allow a student to respond with picture cards, using anchor charts, or following bulleted directions on display. Teacher provided communicative scaffolds during instruction may include extended wait time for ELs to process oral questions or provide comments, rephrasing of the question, or providing a sentence stem for the answer (Kayi-Aydar, 2013). It is important to take into account students' English language proficiency, academic background knowledge and other considerations; otherwise, over relying on routine scaffolds or offering the same supports to all ELs may hold students back in their language development (de Oliveira & Athanases, 2017).

See also: Sociocultural Theory.

de Oliveira, L. C., & Athanases, S. Z. (2017). A framework to reenvision instructional scaffolding for linguistically diverse learners. *Journal of Adolescent & Adult Literacy*, 61(2), 123–129.

Fenner, D. S., & Snyder, S. (2017). *Unlocking English learners' potential: Strategies for making content accessible*. Corwin.

Kayi-Aydar, H. (2013). Scaffolding language learning in an academic ESL classroom. *ELT Journal*, 67(3), 324–335.

Seal of Biliteracy is a U.S. program that recognizes students who gave gained proficiency in more than one language by the time of high school graduation.

The Seal of Biliteracy originated in California with the initiative of Californians Together in response to a critical issue: a significant number of students from minoritized language backgrounds were not developing their home languages given the primarily English-language instruction and curricula, and English-proficient students were not being encouraged to develop multilingualism or multiliteracy. Since the inception of the Seal in 2008, to date, nearly all 50 states in the United States have adopted a similar policy and program to encourage students to attain proficiency in at least two languages by the time they graduate high school (Seal of Biliteracy, n.d.).

Qualifying criteria may include participation in a dual language, bilingual, or heritage language program or world language courses depending on the options available, as well as successful completion of other requirements such as a portfolio, oral presentation, or a standardized language assessment. Most Seals takes the form of a certification that stands as evidence of the student's language proficiency including a seal on the student's high school diploma and transcripts. The recognition highlights students' language abilities when applying to jobs or university programs or placing into additional language courses.

Despite the benefits, some scholars worry that in effect, the Seal alleviates the federal government from the responsibility of instituting a national bilingual education policy (Hancock & Davin, 2021) and that native-born speakers of English tend to be benefited more by the program than students of minoritized language backgrounds (Valdés, 2020).

See also: Bilingual Education Act (BEA), Bilingualism (models of), Language Planning, Language Policy.

Hancock, C. R., & Davin, K. J. (2021). Shifting ideologies: The seal of biliteracy in the United States. In U. Lanvers, A. S. Thompson, & M. East (Eds.), *Language learning in anglophone countries* (pp. 71–88). Palgrave Macmillan.
Seal of Biliteracy. (n.d). *Frequently asked questions*. Seal of Biliteracy. https://sealofbiliteracy.org/
Valdés, G. (2020). The future of the seal of biliteracy: Issues of equity and inclusion. In A. J. Heineke & K. Davis (Eds.), *The seal of biliteracy: Case studies and considerations for policy implementation* (pp. 177–204). Information Age Publishing.

Second Language Acquisition Hypothesis suggests that acquiring a second language is done primarily subconsciously like acquiring a first language.

Through constant exposure to the language, Krashen (1982) argues that we unconsciously acquire the language and the rules of the language without having to consciously learn the grammar, vocabulary, etc. This can be done by immersion in another language orally or by reading articles, books, etc. in the second language.

This hypothesis contrasts with a learning orientation to language, which Krashen labels the "The Acquisition-Learning Distinction" (1982, p. 10). The Second Language Acquisition Hypothesis has its basis in cognitive psychology and generative linguistics. Within the acquisition orientation of language, the communicative method is a prime example. Children learn their first language this way. Other acquisition methods found in classrooms include the Silent Way, Total Physical Response, Natural Approach, Community Language Learning, and Problem Posing. On the other end of the spectrum, the learning viewpoint springs from the empiricist orientation which is based on behavioral psychology and structural linguistics. Grammar translation and the audio-lingual method are prime examples wherein rule learning, memorization, studying, and conscious learning occurs (Freeman & Freeman, 2014). Learning a language and learning about a language primarily takes place in school-based settings. Acquiring a language happens at recess and in the neighborhood with peers.

There is a debate among second language theorists as to whether adults can acquire a new language the way children do or if they must learn it. Those who subscribe to the acquisition hypothesis believe that adults can also acquire a new language. Adults may have more of an accent than those who acquire the new language before puberty, but they can also "take-up" a new language the way a child does (Krashen, 1982).

See also: Community Language Learning (CLL), Natural Approach, Second Language Acquisition Stages, Silent Way, Total Physical Response (TPR).

Freeman, D. E., & Freeman Y. S. (2014). *Essential linguistics: What teachers need to know to teach ESL, reading, spelling, grammar* (2nd ed.). Heinemann.

Krashen, S. (1982). *Principals and practice in second language acquisition*. Permagon Press.

Semantics is a branch of linguistics concerned with the study of meaning.

Making and exchanging meanings involve understanding individual words, how these words function together, and how the speaker and listener make sense of these exchanges in context (Park-Johnson & Shin, 2020).

To effectively communicate, the organization and choice of words, along with their relationship to surrounding words, are critical for conveying the desired meaning. Some miscommunications at the word-level occur due to homophones (words with different spellings and meanings that are pronounced the same as *accept* and *except*) and polysemantic words (words with multiple meanings such as *dull* or *table*). With the help of surrounding words, the meaning of a single word and the larger message can be inferred.

The way in which we arrange words in sentences also contributes to meaning. Syntax, tense, and grammatical patterns link individual words into a larger discernable idea or message. A sentence can be consistent with the grammatical "rules" of a language (e.g., *adjective + subject, verb + adverb*) but not make any sense (e.g., *green ideas sleep furiously*). By the same token, a sentence that does not meet certain grammatical "rules" (e.g., sentence fragments such as *Because he ate dinner*) or vague statements (like *I saw a child on a hill with a telescope*) would add an additional layer of difficulty to interpret the intended meaning.

Meaning is furthermore constructed by the sociocultural setting in which the communication is taking place. Non-linguistic elements such as a speaker's attitude and the perspectives of the speaker and listener play an important role (e.g., saying "sorry" without implying fault as in *I'm sorry your father passed*). In English as in other languages, tone can indicate the end of sentences or whether the speaker is asking a question, or even can convey the speaker's emotions without specifically using words that would otherwise indicate emotion. Additionally, we all come with different backgrounds and our interpretations can be swayed or influenced by preconceived notions (Kramsch, 1998).

See also: Figurative Language, Homonyms, Linguistics, Morphology, Pragmatics.

Kramsch, C. (1998). *Language and culture*. Oxford University Press.
Park-Johnson, S., & Shin, S. J. (2020). *Linguistics for language teachers: Lessons for classroom practice*. Routledge.

Sheltered instruction refers to a teaching framework that integrates content and explicit English language instruction to support the academic success of students simultaneously learning English and content-area subjects at school.

One of the most widely used approaches to sheltered instruction is Sheltered Instruction Observation Protocol (SIOP) (Short & Echevarria, 2008). Teachers who use the SIOP model plan their lessons with content and a related language objective for students to learn. SIOP lessons also encompass other elements including Lesson Preparation, Building Background, Comprehensible Input, Strategies, Interaction, Practice & Application, Lesson Delivery, and Review & Assessment (Echevarria et al., 2008).

SIOP was developed after a 7-year study of middle school classroom teaching practices. The authors compiled the most effective methods into an instructional protocol with various strategies and features that are designed to be taught to content area teachers as part of their professional development in teaching English learners. Several models preceded and laid the foundation for SIOP, such as Cognitive Academic Language Learning Approach (CALLA), differentiated learning and cooperative learning (Hansen-Thomas, 2008). Typical SIOP activities include active classroom discussions, debates, hands-on activities, and cooperative learning activities.

As a program model, sheltered instruction is common in middle and secondary schools where parallel versions of content-area classes (like biology and American history) are tailored to English learners and taught by teachers with expertise in TESOL or ESL. Sheltered instruction is often referred to as Specifically Designed Academic Instruction in English (SDAIE). Within this approach, group work, explicit teaching of learning strategies, and hands-on instruction are emphasized (Hansen-Thomas, 2008).

See also: Language Functions, Newcomer Program, Program Models.

Hansen-Thomas, H. (2008). Sheltered instruction: Best practices for ELLs in the mainstream. *Kappa Delta Pi Record*, 44(4), 165–169.
Short, D. J., Fidelman, C. G., & Louguit, M. (2012). Developing academic language in English language learners through sheltered instruction. *TESOL Quarterly*, 46(2), 334–361.
Vogt, M., & Echevarria, J. (2008). *99 ideas and activities for teaching English learners with the SIOP model* (p. 208). Pearson Allyn and Bacon.
Echevarria, J., Vogt, M., & Short, D. (2008). *Making content comprehensible for English learners: The SIOP model*. Pearson.

Silent period refers to the phase observed in second language acquisition where the learner does not yet produce expressive language (speaking or writing) but is actively processing the additional language (primarily through listening).

The silent period sometimes occurs with English Learners (ELs) who are at a beginning level of second language acquisition with little exposure to English prior to entering school (Wright, 2015). This developmental stage is also known as pre-production for both first and second language acquisition. For English learners, the length of this silent period can last for as little as a few days or up to one year. Sometimes teachers assume ELs are not learning during this stage. That is not true as they are building their receptive language skills like infants learning their first language during their pre-production period. In contrast to infants who may babble during preproduction of their first language, ELs do not babble, but instead employ silence. Teachers need to be aware of this silent period and not misinterpret it as passive aggressive defiance or lack of intelligence. Their receptive language is growing with their comprehension of the English language.

During the silent period, teachers are encouraged to provide non-verbal cues, model the learning desired, use realia, and provide wait time which will help the learner of the language to participate in classroom activities during this period. Wait time refers to the time between the ending of the question and when the student begins to respond. Choral responses by the entire class are also an effective technique to use for those in the silent period.

The concept of the silent period in language acquisition has its roots in Krashen's research (1982) on second language acquisition. However, as with many hypotheses, there are researchers who hold differing viewpoints and critique Krashen's work (Roberts, 2014). Nonetheless, understanding and accommodating the silent period remains valuable for educators working with ELs as they navigate the complexities of acquiring a new language.

See also: Language Domains, Stages of Second Language Acquisition.

Krashen, S. T. (1982). *Principles and practice in second language acquisition*. Pergamon Press.
Roberts, T. A. (2014). Not so silent after all: Examination and analysis of the silent stage in childhood second language acquisition. *Early Childhood Research Quarterly, 29*, 22–40.
Wright, W. (2015). *Foundations for teaching English language learners: Research, theory, policy and practice* (2nd ed.). Caslon.

Silent way entails a manner of teaching in which teacher talk is reduced to promote student concentration and practice of grammatical and lexical lessons with manipulatives.

The silent way is a teaching method in which the teacher remains mostly silent. Students are considered independent learners and have the ability and responsibility to learn the target language by their own realization of rules and without having them being explicitly taught. The silent way was developed by Caleb Gategno, who believed that discovery and problem-solving instead of repetition as well as touchable items enable learning (Richards & Rodgers, 2001). Cuisenaire rods are used to represent grammar structures and vocabulary, while color charts, also known as Fidel charts, are used to represent sounds and pronunciation (Freeman & Freeman, 2014; Richards & Rodgers, 2001). In addition, the teacher may use gestures, mimes, a pointer, and other visual aids to guide students' speaking.

Silent way lessons are basically structured on the gradual presentation of grammar and vocabulary according to their degree of difficulty. Time during every lesson is also dedicated to pronunciation using charts with sound-color associations that later help with spelling and reading. Since students are autonomous, they are expected to draw conclusions, generalize and create rules; therefore, error correction and explanations are deeply inductive as is most of the lesson (Richards & Rodgers, 2001).

Advocates of the silent way say that the teacher's silence helps students concentrate, be alert, and monitor one's error-correction. Although silence is also one of its most distinct features, it is also seen as the most challenging element by most instructors (Richards & Rodgers, 2001). At present, the silent way is used only by a small number of teachers as the primary language teaching methodology (Byram, 2000).

See also: Error Correction.

Byram, M. (2000). *Routledge Encyclopedia of language teaching and learning*. Routledge.
Freeman, D. E., & Freeman Y. S. (2014). *Essential linguistics: What teachers need to know to teach ESL, reading, spelling, grammar* (2nd ed.). Heinemann.
Richards, J. C., & Rodgers, T. S. (2001). *Approaches and methods in language teaching* (2nd ed.). Cambridge University Press.
Richards, J. C., & Schmidt, R. (2010). *Longman dictionary of language teaching and applied linguistics* (4th ed.). Pearson.

Sociocultural theory is a learning theory derived from the work of the Russian psychologist Lev Vygotsky that emphasizes the role of social context in learning.

Within the social context of learning, especially important factors are social relationships (for example, between peers, siblings, or students and teachers) and participation in cultural practices (such as schooling, play time, and family routines) (Lantolf, 2000). Within this perspective, human development is brought about through, rather than requisite to, an individual's social, historical, and cultural experiences.

A key part of Vygotsky's theory is the Zone of Proximal Development (ZOPD). The ZOPD is defined as the space between what a child can do unaided and what a child can accomplish with a more skilled peer or expert. Through these shared activities aided by a more capable peer, children eventually acquire knowledge and skills, as well as physical and psychological tools to promote thinking and learning. In these shared activities, Vygotsky placed special attention on the role of language and other modes of expression as mediating learning (Jon-Steiner & Mahn, 1996).

In the areas of second language acquisition, sociocultural theory emphasizes the role that social interaction plays in learning and the idea that language learning involves communicative activity (Lantolf, 2000). There are several implications that can be derived from a sociocultural perspective for the TESOL or bilingual classroom. Teachers are encouraged to incorporate communicative activities that require students to negotiate meaning with each other. Working together on communicative activities gives students more opportunities to practice theanguagee and make it their own. When this supportive dialogue takes place between a student and a teacher or a more proficient peer it stretches the learner's abilities more so than if they had worked alone.

See also: Assets-Based Pedagogies, Scaffolding.

Jon-Steiner, V., & Mahn, H. (1996). Sociocultural approaches to learning and development: A Vygotskian framework. *Educational Psychologist, 31*, 191–206.
Lantolf, J. P. (2000). Introducing sociocultural theory. In J. P. Lantolf (Ed.), *Sociocultural theory and second language learning*. Oxford University Press.

Stages of second language acquisition are considered broad stages of second language acquisition which have implications for teaching and assessment.

The stages of second language acquisition are based on the early work of Krashen and Terrell (1983). While generic in nature, these stages can be helpful for educators to better understand what can be expected of language learners and progressively design targeted instruction. The stages are often divided into the following five levels and assume a consistent exposure to the target language over time (Herrera & Murray, 2015).

Preproduction is the earliest stage of language acquisition and is also known as pre-speech or the silent period. This period may last from 2 weeks to 2 months. Students in this stage have beginning comprehension and rely heavily on context and visual or gestural cues for understanding.

The Early Production stage may last from about 2–4 months with the oral production of one or two-word responses. Comprehension is emergent. Speech may be disconnected with mispronunciations. The teacher can pair the student with one slightly more advanced and use gestures, graphics and simple commands with bulleted lists.

Speech Emergent may last from 1–2 years with production of simple sentences. Comprehension is good when context is given. Beginning of conversational speech. Some basic grammatical errors are found. The teacher can assist students in utilizing sound letter relationships, pre-teach key vocabulary and concepts. Expand the use of context and graphic clues.

Intermediate Fluency may last from 3 to 5 years and consist of simple and complex sentences. Comprehension is increased and the beginnings of academic language are evident. The teacher should focus on vocabulary and written text in a way that relates to students' prior experiences. Emphasize students' strengths and progress as you give feedback.

Advanced Fluency is the latest stage and consists of abstract thinking expressed in complex language and academic vocabulary. Through exposure to literature, students connect with their life experiences while encountering more complex language construction and figurative language.

See also: English Language Proficiency (ELP), Natural Approach, Second Language Acquisition Hypothesis

Herrera, S. G., & Murray, K. G. (2015). *Mastering ESL and bilingual methods: Differentiated instruction for culturally and linguistically diverse (CLD) students* (3rd ed.). Pearson.

Krashen, S., & Terrell, T. (1983). *The natural approach: Language acquisition in the classroom.* Pergamon.

Students with Limited or Interrupted Formal Education (SLIFE) are considered a subpopulation of students learning English as an additional language at school and who (1) have experienced limited or no formal education or sporadic formal education and (2) are academically two years below their peers.

SLIFE face many of the same academic, economic, and linguistic barriers at school as other English learners, but the interruption of schooling exacerbates these challenges. The lack of consistent schooling in their home countries can be attributed to various factors including political instability, natural disaster, and/or economic insecurity (DeCapua & Marshall, 2015).

It's important to acknowledge that SLIFE students are often immigrants who have experienced education systems significantly different from the standardized curriculum and assessments prevalent in their new host country. Many of them come from cultures that emphasize collectivism (Rothstein-Finch et al., 2009) and rely heavily on oral traditions (Bigelow & Schwarz, 2010). Consequently, SLIFE students may have received their previous education through methods like oral transmission, memorization, and imitation (Flziatz, 2012).

Moreover, SLIFE students entering a new school during adolescence often hail from cultures where they are viewed as capable adults with a range of life skills. In their new educational context, however, they are expected to transition into full-time students within a formal education system that significantly differs from their home country's approach. To effectively engage these students, teachers must adopt a personalized approach that tailors the curriculum to be age-appropriate and directly relevant to the students' lives (Cohen & Honigsfeld, 2017).

See also: English Learner (EL), Newcomer Program.

Bigelow, M., & Schwarz, R. (2010). *Adult English language learners with limited literacy.* National Institute for Adult Literacy.

Cohen, A., & Honigsfeld, A. (2017). Students with Interrupted Formal Education (SIFEs): Actionable practices. *NABE Journal of Research and Practice, 8*(1), 166–175.

DeCapua, A., & Marshall, H. W. (2016). Reframing the conversation about students with limited or interrupted formal education: From achievement gap to cultural dissonance. *NASSP Bulletin, 99*(4), 356–370.

Rothstein-Fisch, C., Trumbull, S., & Garcia, S. (2009). Making the implicit explicit: Supporting teachers to bridge cultures. *Early Childhood Research Quarterly, 24,* 474–486.

Suggestopedia is a teaching technique used to promote language learning by ensuring students feel comfortable and confident through a relaxed classroom atmosphere and physical surroundings.

Suggestopedia emerged in the 1970s as the pedological brainchild of Lozanov (1978), an educator, psychiatrist, and proponent of Suggestology, which combined elements of psychotherapy, neuropsychiatry, and yoga techniques. The basic premise behind suggestopedia is that communication is based on conscious and subconscious responses to stimuli which require interpretation. To increase the learner's capacity for interpretation, music and relaxation techniques are used to create a positive, creative mindset.

A specific type of role play is also used in suggestopedia where teachers create a scenario and students take on a fictitious personality with name, profession, and nationality. The same persona may then be used in subsequent scenarios created by the teacher. This practice reduces self-consciousness and fosters motivation (Shimbo, 2008). While suggestopedia implies students should be actively speaking and listening, in practice, most classrooms using this method result in the teacher primarily talking (Colliander & Fejes, 2021).

While suggestopedia was a prominent pedagogy in language education during the 1970s and 80s, the method has largely fallen out of favor (Stapelton, 2013). However, in more recent years, this method has seen a resurgence in countries in Europe with large immigrant populations, such as Sweden (Colliander & Fejes, 2021). Despite its renewed interest, it's important to note that there is little scientific evidence supporting its efficacy. While suggestopedia incorporates several elements of a sociocultural framework, it lacks a strong emphasis on teachers harnessing students' assets or providing scaffolded support (Colliander & Fejes, 2021).

Colliander, H., & Fejes, A. (2021). The re-emergence of suggestopedia: Teaching a second language to adult migrants in Sweden. *Language, Culture & Curriculum, 34*(1), 51–64.
Lozanov, G. (1978). *Suggestology and the outlines of suggestopedia*. Gordan and Breach.
Stapelton, P. (2013). Using conference submission data to uncover broad trends in language teaching. A case study of one conference over 30 years. *Language Teaching Research, 17*(2), 144–163.

Syntax has to do with the order of words in a sentence.

If it is a simple sentence, it will have one clause such as "Dogs ran." This consists of one noun and one verb. Or we can elaborate and say, "Those lean dogs ran fast." It is still just one clause, but now we have a noun phrase "Those lean dogs" and a verb phrase "ran fast" (Freeman & Freeman, 2014). We have added a determiner and an adjective to the noun and an adverb to the verb.

Languages vary in the placement of adjectives and verbs. In English, the adjective usually comes before the noun and the adverb may be before or after the verb. In contrast, languages like Spanish often place the adjective after the noun. This distinction can leader to challenges for Spanish speakers learning English, potentially resulting in negative transfer.

The placement of words within clauses help second language learners know what type of word an unknown word is. "Jabberwocky" by Lewis Carrol is a good example of a poem with nonsense words that can be made sense of in English using syntax cues. "Twas brillig and the slithy toves." "Twas" is an old-fashioned way of saying "It was" which means we need a noun next to be the object. So we might say, "Twas autumn and the .... "We need another noun phrase. Since it is two words and English puts adjectives before nouns, we need an adjective/noun phrase such as "slimy toads."

Each word or phrase within a sentence serves a semantic function, such as subject or object, contributing to the sentence"s meaning. Syntax, on the other hand, is concerned with the structural arrangement of these elements rather than their semantic roles. Understanding the interplay between syntax and semantics is fundamental to comprehending the form and meaning of language expressions.

See also: Language Functions, Linguistics, Systemic Functional Linguistics (SFL).

Freeman, D. E., & Freeman, Y. S. (2014). *Essential linguistics: What teachers need to know to teach ESL, reading, spelling, grammar* (2nd ed.). Heinemann.

Systemic Functional Linguistics (SFL) is a meaning-focused view of language that includes a framework to analyze language and implications for practice.

Systemic Functional Linguistics views language as a resource for meaning. Developed by Michael Halliday to address language discrimination (Harman, 2018), SFL is sensitive to social context and prioritizes effectiveness of language choices within a particular context, over a singular style of correctness.

SFL analyzes language based on three factors that shape the context: *field*, the topic or subject matter; *tenor*, the roles, relationships, and power dynamics; and *mode*, the channel of communication. For example, in a science class where students brainstorm climate change projects, the *field* is climate change, the *tenor* are students in small groups, and the *mode* is oral conversation. Together, *field* (the what), *tenor* (the who), and *mode* (the how) combine to construct a particular *register*. The register in this example is formal to the degree that students are discussing a scientific topic, but at the same time somewhat informal because students are having an oral conversation. If one element changes (e.g., instead of discussing climate change, students discuss their weekend plans, or instead of brainstorming, they now prepare some written notes, so does the register.

Within SFL, lexical and grammatical resources explain how patterns of meaning function in text (Martin & Rose, 2003). An SFL-informed pedagogy, involves, for example, how circumstances (or adverbs and prepositional phrases) can add detail to an action, or how referents (especially pronouns) and synonyms (words with similar meanings) can create cohesion in a text by avoiding unnecessary repetition and help the reader track people and ideas as the text unfolds (Derewianka, 2011). This approach encourages students to derive patterns from examples, make purpose-driven language choices, and develop familiarity with metalanguage (de Oliveira & Schleppegrell, 2016).

See also: Academic Language, Genre, Language Functions, Linguistics, Syntax.

de Oliveira, L. C., & Schaleppegrell, M. J. (2016). *Focus on grammar and meaning.* Oxford University Press.

Derewianka, B. M. (2011). *A new grammar companion for teachers.* Primary English Teaching Association Australia.

Harman, R. (Ed.). (2018). *Bilingual learners and social equity: Critical approaches to systemic functional linguistics.* Springer.

Martin, J. R., & Rose, D. (2003). *Working with discourse: Meaning beyond the clause.* Bloomsbury Publishing.

Task-Based Language Teaching is an approach that brings meaningful and interactive tasks to students, and to complete those, students have to be involved in real communication and negotiation.

Within Task-Based Language Teaching (TBLT), also known as Task-Based Instruction (TBI), tasks can be *real-world tasks* or *authentic pedagogical tasks*. Learners are required to use in class the language that they would use in real life or relevant to real-world situations. Learning tasks might be real-life rehearsals (e.g., how to use the phone) or pedagogical (e.g., information gap activity). Pedagogical tasks do not exactly mirror real-life activities but do fulfill a class or lesson purpose to promote language learning (Nunan, 1989; Richards & Rodgers, 2001). In TBLT the idea is that the grammatical forms will be acquired without overt instruction because learners are using the language authentically to accomplish meaningful and result-driven tasks. Even though defining a "task" may vary within TBLT, a shared view is that a task must be achieved through successful language use. Tasks are also motivating for several reasons. First, they comprise teamwork and may naturally incorporate body movements. Also, tasks invite learners to share previous experiences, and therefore tasks welcome diverse ways of expressing oneself (Richards & Rodgers, 2001).

According to its advocates, TBLT promotes language learning beyond simply comprehending the language since learners will have to negotiate meaning and join a more natural and realistic interaction to complete the tasks. Being able to produce language output and not only comprehending input is crucial for language development to occur. This can be done while students have conversations to, for instance, negotiate meaning or plan tasks and their respective performances. Having tasks at the core of planning lessons to promote language input-output is what differentiates TBLT from other teaching methods and approaches. TBLT's focus is primarily on the on the journey or process and not necessarily on the destination or product (Richards & Rodgers, 2001).

See also: Communicative Language Teaching (CLT).

Nunan, D. (1989). *Designing tasks for the communicative classroom*. Cambridge University Press.
Richards, J. C., & Rodgers, T. S. (2001). *Approaches and methods in language teaching* (2nd ed.). Cambridge University Press.

Total Physical Response (TPR) is a teaching method based on the hypothesis that people learn language better in a stress-free environment in which they respond to comprehensible input by using bodily movement and gestures.

TPR was especially popular in the 1970s and 80s. Within this approach, students may be asked, for example, to touch or point to objects or pictures that correspond to the response the teacher is expecting or to vocabulary words being called out. Often, this approach combines actions that involve imperative verbs (commands) and vocabulary (e.g., "open the book"). TPR is considered effective for students to demonstrate their comprehension of input. Therefore, oral comprehension is the major goal of TPR, while speaking is supposed to happen only if students feel ready and comfortable to do so (Richards & Rodgers, 2001).

An essential concept within TPR is the active filter hypothesis (Krashen, 1981). According to this hypothesis, language acquisition is more successful or likely in stress-free settings, which can be challenging for adults learning an additional language. In this regard, TPR aims to recreate a natural and comfortable environment reminiscent of childhood language acquisition. Linking physical movements to understandable language input allows relaxed students to fully focus on learning without feeling self-conscious.

Even though TPR is mostly considered for beginners and children, it can be used with students of all ages and levels of English. Like other methods, teachers may choose TPR activities or lessons for storytelling, content-based vocabulary, songs, chants, and poems to name a few (Peck, 2001). It is also often recommended that TPR be a part of a lesson that will incorporate other teaching methods and approaches instead of being used by itself.

See also: Active Filter Hypothesis, Comprehensible Input Hypothesis, Second Language Acquisition Hypothesis.

Krashen, S. D. (1981). *Second language acquisition and second language learning.* Pergamon Press.
Peck, S. (2001). Developing children's listening and speaking skills in ESL. In M. Celce-Murcia (Ed.), *Teaching English as second or foreign language* (3rd ed., pp. 139–149). Heinle & Heinle.
Richards, J. C., & Rodgers, T. S. (2001). *Approaches and methods in language teaching* (2nd ed.). Cambridge University Press.

Translanguaging involves the use of multiple languages and registers, sometimes in the same conversation or utterance, to effectively communicate or complete a task.

Translanguaging is a common linguistic practice among bilinguals and represents a holistic approach to bilingual education and research (Goodman, & Tastanbek, 2021). In contrast to monolingual models that tend to view languages as separate and static, translanguaging emphasizes that bilinguals use their languages and language varieties flexibly and dynamically within an *integrated system* (García & Wei, 2014). For example, in class, a bilingual child might perform mental calculations or discuss a topic with peers using the home language, and then the next moment orally share with the class or write a response in the language of instruction. Pedagogy oriented to translanguaging, or "translanguaging as a pedagogical tool" guides and elevates these complex and dynamic linguistic practices. When teachers model translanguaging in their own speech or through the texts they select, they provide guidance and create opportunities for students to comprehend, synthesize, and evaluate information creatively and critically (Celic & Seltzer, 2012).

Even monolingual teachers can promote translanguaging. These teachers can encourage students to use their home languages, make comparisons between languages and linguistic styles, and consider factors such as the audience and purpose in spoken and written grade-level texts. In instances like these, content learning, language development in both languages, and metalinguistic awareness (including knowledge about one's own language) are all supported. As a pedagogical tool, translanguaging contests notions about language separation in bilingual education programs and promotes the strategic use of children and youth's complete linguistic repertoires.

See also: Code switching, Common Underlying Proficiency (CUP).

Celic, C., & Seltzer, K. (2012). *Translanguaging: A CUNY-NYSIEB guide for educators.* https://www.wortreich-sprachbildung.de/fileadmin/wortreich_media/Download/Handreichung_Translanguaging.pdf

García, O., & Wei, L. (2014). *Translanguaging: Language, bilingualism and education.* Palgrave MacMillan.

Goodman, B., & Tastanbek, S. (2021). Making the shift from a codeswitching to a translanguaging lens in English language teacher education. *TESOL Quarterly, 55*(1), 29–53.

Universal Grammar (UG) refers to a theory by Noam Chomsky who proposed that all humans are born with the mental structures to subconsciously form rules for how language works, which facilitates the innate ability to learn and use language.

Although languages differ, all languages have rules. UG encompasses what all languages have in common. Children are not born with knowledge specific to one language or another like Vietnamese or English. Children are born with knowledge of the things that span across languages and this knowledge is what gives humans the internal and natural capability for language and language learning, regardless of what language that is.

UG encompasses not only syntax but also the other fundamental aspects of language including, phonology, morphology, semantics, and pragmatics. Chomsky's views help to explain why even though certain structures are uncommon, and children are rarely exposed to them, they are still able to develop and use those grammatical structures accurately. Said differently, we don't have to be exposed to every single way of making an utterance to produce it. Universal Grammar is what supports our generative capacity to produce language (Scarcella & Oxford, 1992).

UG is a theory that helps explain first or native language acquisition, although some scholars make connections between UG and second language learning. Within an acquisition-based view of second language development, as with native language acquisition, little attention is placed on explicit grammar teaching and error correction (Lightbown & Spada, 2013; White, 2003). It can be useful for educators to be familiar with these theories to understand and treat learner errors as an indispensable part of their language development as errors reflect learners' creativity to produce language because of their innate grammar competence (Scarcella & Oxford, 1992).

See also: Interlanguage, Natural Order Hypothesis.

Lightbown, P. M., & Spada, N. (2013). *How languages are learned* (4th ed.). Oxford University Press.
Scarcella, R. C., & Oxford, R. L. (1992). *The tapestry of language learning.* Heinle & Heinle.
White, L. (1985). The acquisition of parameterized grammars: Subjacency in second language acquisition. *Second Language Research, 1,* 1–17.
White, L. (2003). *Second language acquisition and universal grammar.* Cambridge University Press.

U.S. School Procedures for Identification and Services for English Learners
ensure eligibility for educational services.

For students to qualify for English language services, there are certain procedures. The following stages describe the trajectory involving how a student is identified to receive and eventually transition out of services.

Identification of a potential English learner (EL) begins when a student registers in a PK-12 school, and the parents (or guardians) are asked to complete a Home Language Survey. The survey normally asks what language the student primarily uses at home. If the parent lists a language besides English, the student is given an English Language Proficiency screener. In schools that offer a bilingual program, the student may also be given proficiency test in the students' dominant language (Bailey & Kelly, 2013). This screening determines the pool of potential ELs.

Classification entails determining the student's level of English language proficiency (ELP) through a state adopted ELP Assessment or screener. At this point, the student receives an initial classification of EL or initially fluent English proficient (or I-FEP), or non-EL (Linquanti & Cook, 2013). If the student is classified as an EL, the current ELP level is also determined.

ELP Assessment and Monitoring involves a performance standard which defines English proficiency and the levels leading to proficiency. Per federal law, ELs must be testing annually in four domains for English proficiency—reading, writing, listening and speaking. The law also requires states to measure progress. Common assessments used to determine these levels are WIDA and ELPA 21.

Reclassification may result in exiting a student from EL status and services into former EL status where the student must be monitored. This decision is based on assessment results required by ESEA Title III and other criteria such as classroom performance required by ESEA Title I (Linquanti & Cook, 2013).

See also: English Language Proficiency (ELP), English Language Proficiency Standards, English Learner, Language Planning, Language Policy

Bailey, A. L., & Kelly, K. R. (2013). Home language survey practices in the initial identification of English learners in the United States. *Educational Policy, 27*(5), 770–804.
Linquanti, R. & Cook, H. G. (2013). Toward a "common definition of English learner:" Guidance for states and state assessment consortia in defining and addressing policy and technical issues and options. Council of Chief State School Officers. https://files.eric.ed.gov/fulltext/ED565753.pdf

Vocabulary teaching and learning refer here to the systematic teaching of words and word parts to enhance language development.

The approach to teaching and learning vocabulary has evolved from translation and isolated learning to contextual understanding. This includes considering a word's collocations, forms, register, spelling, and pronunciation. For instance, learning 'success' involves understanding related words like 'succeed,' 'successful,' and 'successfully,' along with collocations such as 'to be successful at.' Acquiring this deep knowledge may require up to 40 meaningful exposures (Lems et al., 2017).

Teaching and learning vocabulary involves three types of strategies: Specific word instruction, word-learning strategies, and word consciousness (Honig et al., 2018). Specific word instruction involves direct teaching of vocabulary, utilizing the Three-Tier System. Tier I includes common spoken words (e.g., ball, baby, happy), Tier II comprises academic words used across content areas (e.g., transport, judge, classify), and Tier III consists of discipline-specific academic words (e.g., photosynthesis in science or filibuster in U.S. government) (Beck et al., 2002). The deliberate effort required for teaching and learning Tier 2 and 3 words sets them apart from Tier 1 words.

Word-learning strategies, including root word analysis and understanding affixes like prefixes and suffixes, help students become independent word users. Root words, the foundation of many words, can be explored to derive meanings. Common prefixes like un, re, in, and dis cover approximately 58% of prefixed words (Honig et al., 2018). Focusing on root words is particularly beneficial for students speaking Romance languages. Additionally, teaching cognates, words similar in English to a student's home language, is another effective word-learning strategy.

Word consciousness, an awareness and interest in words, enhances students' word skills. Teachers can nurture word consciousness by creating a language-rich environment with resources like word walls, games, literature, read-alouds, wordplay, and joke books (Honig et al., 2018).

See also: Academic Language, Cognates, Morphology

Beck, I., McKeown, M., & Kucan, L. (2002). *Bringing words to life*. Guilford Press.
Honig, B. Diamond, L. & Gutlohn, L. (2018). *Teaching reading sourcebook* (3rd ed.). CORE and Arena Press.
Lems, K., Miller, L. D., & Soro, T. M. (2017). *Building literacy with English language learners: Insights from linguistics*. Guilford Publications.

World Englishes is the concept that the English language is diverse with many international varieties.

While English has often been considered a global language, this internationality has historically been primarily associated with what is commonly referred to as Standard English, which is often dominated by American or British English. Consequently, the traditional definition of English, especially Standard English, did not fully account for its global diversity and plurality. To illustrate, individuals from Canada, Ireland, or Nigeria may have distinct perceptions of what constitutes Standard English (Farrell & Martin, 2009).

Braj Kachru was the first linguist to introduce the idea of World Englishes to the TESOL field. He conducted extensive research into the multitude of English varieties worldwide, extending beyond the confines of English as spoken by native users of the language (Alatis, 2005). Kachru's notable work includes the development of the Concentric Circles of English, also known as the Kachruvian three-circle model, categorizing English into inner (first language), outer (second language), and expanding circles, foreign language (Kachru, 1996).

In recent decades, Kachru's Three Concentric Circles Model has stirred debates. While some see it as influential, critics argue it oversimplifies English variations. Regardless, the Kachruvian Model significantly contributes to TESOL and our understanding of English's global evolution (Al-Mutairi, 2020).

Today, World Englishes has evolved from being a theoretical concept or ideology within the TESOL field. Its ideals of inclusion and avoiding the homogenization of English have been increasingly accepted and embraced worldwide. Questioning the notion of standard English while contrasting it to World Englishes is an invaluable role for TESOL professionals.

See also: L1 and L2, Native Speaker (NS) and Nonnative Speaker (NNS)

Alatis, J. E. (2005). Kachru's circles and the growth of professionalism in TESOL. *English Today*, 82(21), 25–34.

Al-Mutairi, M. A. (2020). Kachru's three concentric circles model of English language: An overview of criticism & the place of Kuwait in it. *English Language Teaching*, 13(1), 85–88. http://dx.doi.org/10.5539/elt.v13n1p85

Farrel, T. S. C., & Martin S. (2009). To teach standard English or world Englishes? A balanced approach to Instruction. *English Teaching Forum*, 2, 2–7.

Kachru, B. B. (1996). World Englishes: Agony and ecstasy. *The Journal of Aesthetic Education*, 30(2), 135–155.

APPENDIX A

TESOL and Bilingual Education Organizations

American Council on the Teaching of Foreign Languages (ACTFL; https://www.actfl.org/)
The American Council on the Teaching of Foreign Languages (ACTFL) is a prominent organization devoted to the advancement of world language education in the United States. Established in 1967, ACTFL has played a central role in shaping language teaching and learning practices. The organization serves as a vital resource for educators, offering guidance, research, and professional development opportunities to enhance language instruction. By promoting proficiency-based approaches and advocating for the value of language skills in an increasingly globalized world, ACTFL contributes significantly to the development of effective language programs and the cultivation of a multilingual and culturally diverse society.

American Association for Applied Linguistics (AAAL; https://www.aaal.org/)
The American Association for Applied Linguistics (AAAL) is a distinguished organization dedicated to the field of applied linguistics. Established in 1977, AAAL has been a driving force in advancing research, scholarship, and practice in linguistics as it applies to real-world contexts. The association provides a platform for scholars, educators, and professionals to collaborate and share knowledge about language-related issues in various sectors, such as education, language policy, and communication. With its commitment to bridging the gap between theory and practical application, AAAL plays a pivotal role in addressing societal challenges related to language diversity, communication, and language education, making it a vital resource in the field of applied linguistics.

British Council (https://learnenglish.britishcouncil.org/)
The British Council is a globally renowned organization that specializes in international cultural and educational opportunities. Established in 1934, the British Council has been at the forefront of promoting British culture, language, and education worldwide. With a presence in over 100 countries, it offers a wide range of programs and services, including English language teaching, cultural exchange initiatives, and academic partnerships. Through its dedication to fostering connections and mutual understanding between people and cultures, the British Council plays serves an important role in building bridges and promoting a more interconnected and culturally diverse world.

Center for Applied Linguistics (CAL; *https://www.cal.org/*)
The Center for Applied Linguistics (CAL) is a renowned organization committed to advancing the field of applied linguistics. Founded in 1959, CAL has been a leading force in language research, education, and assessment. The organization serves as a hub for linguists, educators, and researchers, offering expertise and resources in areas such as language policy, bilingual education, and language assessment. Through its dedication to promoting linguistic diversity and effective language education, CAL plays a pivotal role in shaping language-related practices, policies, and research to benefit communities and individuals around the world.

The Council of Indigenous Language Organizations
(CILO; *https://www.cilo.world*)
The Council of Indigenous Language Organizations (CILO) is a collective of Indigenous organizations committed to preserving and revitalizing Indigenous languages. They advocate for policies and funding to support language preservation, engage with various stakeholders, and develop educational resources. CILO recognizes the interconnectedness of language and culture, aiming to preserve both. Their efforts include language revitalization, cultural preservation, educational initiatives, and research and documentation projects.

International Association of Teachers of English as a Foreign Language
(IATEFL; *https://www.iatefl.org/*)
The International Association of Teachers of English as a Foreign Language (IATEFL) is a prestigious organization dedicated to the field of English language teaching and learning. Established in 1967, IATEFL has been a prominent advocate for excellence in English language education worldwide. The association serves as a vibrant community for English language educators, offering professional development opportunities, resources, and a platform for sharing innovative teaching practices. With its commitment to fostering effective language education and promoting cross-cultural communication, IATEFL continues to play a pivotal role in enhancing the quality of English language instruction and supporting educators in their efforts to empower learners globally.

International Association for World Englishes (*http://www.iaweworks.org/*)
The International Association for World Englishes (IAWE) is an organization that focuses on the study and promotion of World Englishes. IAWE serves as a platform for scholars, researchers, educators, and language enthusiasts who

are interested in exploring the sociolinguistic and cultural aspects of English as a global language. The organization conducts conferences, publishes research, and facilitates discussions and collaborations among its members to deepen the understanding of how English functions in different regions and communities worldwide. With its focus on World Englishes, IAWE contributes to a broader awareness of linguistic diversity, cultural richness, and the evolving nature of the English language, reflecting its global impact and significance.

Modern Languages Association (MLA; https://www.mla.org/)

The Modern Language Association (MLA) is a renowned organization dedicated to the study and promotion of languages and literatures. Founded in 1883, the MLA has been at the forefront of research and scholarship in the humanities, with a particular focus on languages, literature, and related fields. The association serves as a resource for scholars, educators, and students by providing resources, publications, and conferences that facilitate intellectual exchange and collaboration. Committed to advancing the study and teaching of language and literature, the MLA plays a pivotal role in shaping academic discourse, fostering cultural understanding, and enriching the educational experience for individuals worldwide.

National Association for Bilingual Education (NABE; https://nabe.org/)

The National Association for Bilingual Education (NABE) is a prominent organization dedicated to promoting bilingual and multilingual education in the United States. Established in 1975, NABE has been a leading advocate for policies and practices that support language diversity and equity in education. NABE provides a platform for educators, policymakers, and researchers to collaborate and share knowledge about effective bilingual education strategies. With a commitment to fostering cultural and linguistic inclusivity, NABE plays a crucial role in shaping the landscape of bilingual education in the United States, ensuring that all students have access to quality educational opportunities that embrace their linguistic heritage and contribute to their academic success. There are affiliate organizations in many U.S. states as well as international affiliates in Argentina, China, and Mexico.

TESOL International (https://www.tesol.org/)

TESOL International is a prominent organization dedicated to advancing the field of Teaching English to Speakers of Other Languages (TESOL). With a rich history dating back to 1966, it has consistently played a pivotal role in promoting effective language teaching and learning worldwide. TESOL International offers a wide range of resources, professional development opportunities, and a supportive community for educators and researchers in the TESOL field. Through its commitment to fostering excellence in English language education, TESOL International continues to be a global leader in promoting linguistic diversity and cross-cultural understanding. TESOL International has numerous local affiliate organizations in most U.S. states and numerous countries around the world.

Printed in the United States
by Baker & Taylor Publisher Services